Refugee Dilemma

Refugee Dilemma

Sri Lankan Refugees in Tamil Nadu

V. Suryanarayan

PRABHAT PRAKASHAN

Antar Rashtriya Sahayog Parishad
arspindia@gmail.com

Published by
PRABHAT PRAKASHAN PVT. LTD.
4/19 Asaf Ali Road,
New Delhi-110 002 (INDIA)
e-mail: prabhatbooks@gmail.com

ISBN 978-93-5322-145-4
REFUGEE DILEMMA
by V. Suryanarayan

Edition
2025

Price
₹ 250.00 (Rupees Two Hundred Fifty only)

Printed at
Shree Sai Printers, Sahibabad

To
My sisters
Parvathy (Kunju)
and
Thankam

Acknowledgements

Over the years, I have accumulated several debts. It is very difficult to name all of them. But I will be failing in my duty if I do not refer to important organizations and individuals.

Since 1983, I have interacted with several refugees, both living in the camps and outside. They shared with me their life stories, their trials and tribulations, their hopes and fears. I developed admiration for their resilience against heavy odds. The NGOs working among them - OfERR, Jesuit Refugee Service and ADRA – shared research materials and also their views on several issues relating to refugee presence in Tamil Nadu.

The officials of the UNHCR Office in Chennai have been uniformly kind and considerate. I must make a special mention of Mr. Satchithananantha Valan Michael, Head of the Chennai office, for his encouragement and support at every stage in the preparation of the manuscript. His junior colleagues also helped me identify the photographs.

Mr. K. Subrahamniam and Ambassador M. Ganapathy edited the manuscript and made it readable. My heartfelt thanks to them.

I am deeply indebted to *Antar Rashtriya Sahayog Parishad* for sponsoring the book. It is a pleasure working with Mr. Shyam Parande, Ambassador Virendra Gupta, Ambassador

Anup Mudgal, Ambassador Dayakar, Mr. Sushil Pandit and others who are doing yeoman service in promoting India's relations with its neighbours. Prabhat Prakashan with characteristic efficiency has printed the book. My thanks to Mr. Prabhat Kumar and his diligent colleagues.

Others who deserve special mention and thanks include Dr. Ashik Bonofer, Prof. Bernard Samy, Prof. A. Louie Albert, SJ and Mr. Sandeep Kumar. Mr. Prem Kumar and Ms. Usha Alagappan of the American Library assisted me in locating valuable reference materials. Mrs. Subbalakshmi was always there to share my joys and sorrows. Without her loving care and affection, the book would not have seen the light of the day.

Preface

I, along with Prof V. Sudarsen (late), wrote a book, entitled *Between Fear and Hope: Sri Lankan Refugees in Tamil Nadu* (T.R. Publishers, Chennai, 2000). The publication was sponsored by the UNHCR. Augustine P. Mahiga, then Chief of Mission, UNHCR, sent a message which was included in the book. The book was received with critical acclaim, both in India and abroad.

Much water has flowed through the Palk Strait since then. The Liberation Tigers of Tamil Eelam (LTTE) has been decimated. The Sri Lankan Government has restored law and order and there is apparent calm in the country. Popularly elected governments have assumed power in the northern and eastern provinces. However, the solemn promise made by the President that he would take immediate steps to devolve powers to the Tamil provinces has not been fulfilled. What is more, there is no hope of ethnic reconciliation. While few refugees have returned to the island, majority still prefer to remain in Tamil Nadu.

My friends and well-wishers have suggested that I should bring out a revised and updated version of the book. I have heeded to their request. The result is this book. *Refugee Dilemma – Sri Lankan Refugees in Tamil Nadu* (New Delhi, 2018). Some parts of the earlier book have been retained; but major portions have been updated and written anew.

I am happy that the *Antar Rashtriya Sahayog Parishad* has sponsored the book.

The book chronicles the dilemma faced by the Sri Lankan refugees in the backdrop of the burgeoning number of refugees across the world. It highlights India's tradition of according welcome to refugees and asylum seekers from very early times and describes how New Delhi successfully tackled the flow of millions of refugees since the dawn of independence. The twists and turns in India's Sri Lanka policy have been analysed in detail. The domestic developments in Sri Lanka, before, during and after the end of ethnic conflict, have been addressed. Life in the refugee camps and earlier attempts at repatriation of refugees have been described. What is more, the proposed amendment to the Citizenship Act, 1955 and its implications for Sri Lankan refugees have been critically examined.

The Government of Tamil Nadu every year submits a Policy Note in the Legislative Assembly which gives details of the refugee situation. The Policy Note does not take cognizance of refugees belonging to other nationalities - Tibetan students who pursue higher education, the Rohingyas who live in a camp in Kelambakkam in the Kancheepuram district, Iraqis, Somalians, Sudanese and Yemenese. Since the focus of the book is on the dilemma faced by Sri Lankan refugees, I have not touched upon the problems and prospects of refugees belonging to other nationalities.

Needless to say, the views expressed in the book are mine. And, if there are any shortcomings and omissions, I am responsible.

The book is dedicated to my sisters Parvathy (Kunju) and Thankam.

—V. Suryanarayan

Contents

1
The Refugee Phenomenon

> Wanderers, wanderers we are from land to land do we wander driven by hunger and by death embittered by suffering and pain over sea and hill and plain we outcasts of the earth.
>
> **—Schloime Ansky**

In Swahili language, the term for refugee is *Mkimbizi,* which literally means "a person who runs". In his thought-provoking essay on Burundi refugees in Dar es Salam, Marc Sommers points out that many express disgust at the continued use of the "refugee label" even after two decades of exile. Some believe that "being *Mkimbizi* not only identifies them as people who were compelled to flee their homeland in fear of their survival, but who continue to flee."

The changes taking place across the world reflect the worsening of the refugee situation. In its annual report to mark the World Refugee Day, the UNHCR said that in 2015, for the first time, refugees worldwide had passed the 50 million mark. On an average "24 people were displaced from their homes every minute of every day during 2015 – some 34,000 people every day". Speaking about the largest refugee crisis of our times, Ban Ki Moon, the former UN Secretary-

General, described it "not just a crisis of numbers", but "as a crisis of solidarity". Political turmoil in Syria, Afghanistan, Lake Chad, South Sudan, Somalia, Libya and Myanmar have displaced more than 23 million people – more than the population of 48 US States.

Edward Said, in his book *Culture and Imperialism,* has pointed out that it is one of the "unhappiest characteristics of the age to have produced more refugees, migrants, displaced persons and exiles than ever before in history". As Geetha Ganapathy-Dore has described, they are the "victims of climate change, ethnic cleansing, armed conflict, family, religious or state repression, real estate or rehabilitation projects, or merely poverty and hunger."

The refugee crisis, as Mercy Corps, has underlined "is a human crisis. Behind the statistics are people filled with unique life experiences and dreams for the future. They are mothers longing to return home, fathers yearning to work again, children searching for a childhood". The figures are heart-rending – Syria- 11.5 million; South Sudan – 4 million; Afghanistan – 3.8 million; Lake Chad – 2.8 million; and Somalia – 1.6 million. Filippo Grandi, the UN High Commissioner for Refugees, addressing the United Nations had urged the international community to find political solutions to the world's conflicts "if the swelling numbers of forcibly displaced people are ever to return home".

In his Nadim Makdisi Memorial Lecture delivered in the American University of Beirut, Vijay Prasad has graphically described the refugee trauma in the Middle East. To quote:

> To get to Libya, the migrants and refugees have to cross the Sahara desert, a journey in a pick-up truck takes three days at least. It is perilous. There refugees would die of dehydration. The Sahara is vast, hot and

dangerous...caravans prefer buses, pick-up trucks and jeeps to ferry humans and cocaine towards Europe; guns and money southwards. These newer caravans drive along unmarked paths, heading between sand dunes, searching for old tyre tracks that have been buried in the disorienting sand storms. The migrants huddle in the trucks. They are wearing sun glasses, their only defense in the desert. No proper account exists of dead refugees. When a boat sinks in the Mediterranean Sea, it is within sight of Europe. When refugees die in the desert, no one seems to care.

People of Concern to UNHCR

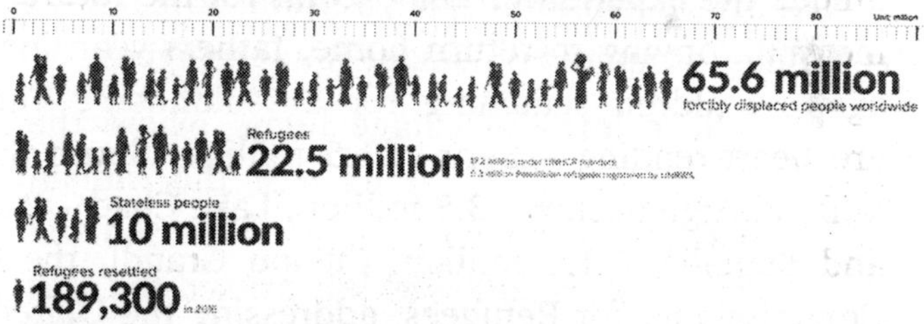

Source: http://www.unhcr.org/figures-at-a-glance.html

Refugee Generating Countries

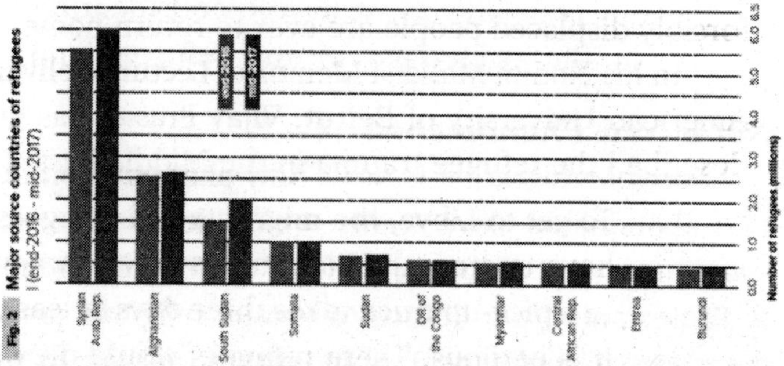

Source:http://www.unhcr.org/statistics/unhcrstats/5aaa4fd27/mid-year-trends-june-2017.html

Being a Refugee

Being a refugee is one of the most tragic experiences in life. It forcibly separates one from familiar surroundings, from near and dear ones and leads to a gloomy feeling of estrangement. As an Iranian refugee in Canada put it, "Exile like death, but without death's ultimate mercy" has torn millions of people from the nourishment of tradition, family and geography". Ezat Mossalanejad has graphically described how the refugees are used as scapegoats for all the socio-economic shortcomings of the host society. What the Greek dramatist Aeschylus wrote in 403 BC, holds true even after the lapse of 2,500 years. To quote Aeschylus, "Everybody is quick to blame aliens. This awkward situation creates impassable barriers for exiles in their attempts to participate in the social life of the host countries".

The Sri Lankan Tamil poet, Selvam, poignantly expresses the feelings of many Sri Lankan Tamil refugees:

> I have lost the village home where the sparrows will build its nest the cadijan leaves will sing with the wind the sun will enter the shoe flower. We crossed the seas dreaming of wealth and a house with a beach in front and a garden along the red soil pathway alas, we have lost our identities in the wilderness of the refugee land.

Not a New Phenomenon

Forcible migration is not a new phenomenon in history. The abominable slave trade, which deprived Africa of its "human resources", but "enriched" the Whites; the migration of Protestants from France to escape religious persecution; the massive deployment of indentured labour to fulfill the demands of expanding colonial economies; the World Wars which triggered refugee movements and forced repatriation – all are illustrations of man's inhumanity to man. During the nineteenth and early twentieth century, the inter-continental migration from the Old to the New World involved some 50 million people, many of whom were "fleeing from persecution in Europe". Between 1945 and 1970, nearly 100 million people were uprooted, "a period, heightened by those displaced in Europe by the Second World War and its aftermath; the partition of India, the division of Germany, the Palestinian Diaspora, the flight of Cubans; the consequences of Indo-Pakistani War and the birth of Bangladesh". Boutros Ghali, the former UN Secretary General, had pointed out: "Refugees and other uprooted people are the products of failure – failure to resolve conflict and its underlying causes – intolerance, antagonism and poverty".

Problem – Likely to Worsen

Economic and political trends indicate to an increase in forced migration of people in the years ahead, not a lessening of it. The pressure of population, economic necessity and environmental degradation will become more compelling reasons for people to leave their communities. What is more, given the endemic nature of armed conflicts and "ethnic cleansing" taking place in different parts of the world, the travails of the refugees are likely to get further compounded in the years to come.

The refugee phenomenon and the response of the host countries are inextricably interwoven with Cold War politics. During the first Cold War, as far as the "free world" was concerned, refugees from communist countries were welcome, because they had a propaganda value. In fact, refugees from communist countries had special aura in the

United States. As Gil Loescher has mentioned, the anti-communist bias in the United States refugee policy got "translated into virtually open-ended blanket admissions for individuals fleeing from communist regimes". Of the 71,303 refugees admitted into the United States during the Reagan administration, 96 per cent were from communist countries. For many years, West Germany provided financial incentives for refugees from East Germany, Romania, and Soviet Union.

The political exploitation of refugees becomes evident if we analyse the backdrop to the external involvement in the Third Indo-China War and the civil war in Afghanistan. The single-minded determination to isolate and ostracise Vietnam paved the way for convergence of interests among the United States, China and member states of ASEAN. The genocide during the Ieng Sary-Pol Pot regime became a forgotten chapter. The Khmer refugees in the refugee camps in the Thailand-Cambodia border were financed, trained and armed to carry on the struggle against the Heng Samrin regime. Keng Sethol, a Khmer refugee, pointed out the final outcome. To quote Keng Sethol, "When the forest burns, the flames are extinguished quickly because the people worry about the burning of forests. But when my country burns with the smoke of war, nobody puts out the fire". In the same way, contending factions in Afghanistan became the surrogates of super powers. The three million Afghan refugees in Pakistan became the reservoir from which the *Mujahidin* recruited its cadres. As is well known, the war machine of the *Mujahidin* was financed and fuelled by the United States and its client state Pakistan.

The Cold War has ended, but the refugee phenomenon continues unabated. As mentioned earlier, Syria, South Sudan, Lake Chad, Afghanistan, Somalia, Libya and

Myanmar - all these countries continue to be trouble spots. What is more painful, most of the asylum giving countries have started to adopt a rigid stance on refugee issues. Former British Prime Minister John Major stated a few years ago, "we must not be wide open in all corners, just because Rome, Paris, and London are more attractive than Bombay or Algiers". When the boat people, mainly ethnic Chinese, began to pour into Southeast Asian countries, Singapore, a Chinese majority state, dissuaded them from entering the city state. Even those countries which advocate an open economic system, free trade and unbridled entry of foreign capital maintain a strict vigil over the entry of asylum-seeking refugees. Western Governments, as Gil Loescher has pointed out, "are now imposing visa requirements, detaining some asylum seekers in centers at airports, or nearby, applying sanctions against airlines and carriers that transport asylum seekers and interpreting the refugee conventions in very restrictive ways. Several European countries have tightened their immigration and asylum laws to restrict further the opportunities for asylum seekers to apply for protection and assistance within Europe". Australia, which is a country of immigrants and has gained immensely from the refugees who have become Australian citizens, has started adopting an inhuman approach towards asylum seekers from Asian countries. The attitude of the general public is also lukewarm. They do not want refugees speaking alien languages and following different customs; they resent the fact that the refugees bring their political squabbles with them. It must also be highlighted that some desperate refugees take advantage of the liberal immigration laws of Switzerland, Germany and Canada. Christopher McDowell has pointed out that many governments feel that the asylum rules are "being abused". As a result, many refugees are perceived as illegal immigrants, as a burden to be avoided.

W.H. Auden graphically describes the tragic plight of the refugees in his poem, ***Refugee Blues:***

> Say this city has ten million souls, Some are living in mansions, Some are living in holes; Yet there is no place for us, My dear, there is no place for us Once we had a country, and we thought it fair, Look in the Atlas and you will find it there; We cannot go there now, my dear, We cannot go there now.

When the Conservative Government decided not to allow lone refugee children a safe haven in the UK, Nicola Davies, the Children's Author, wrote the following lines:

> War took everything War took everyone I was ragged, bloody, all alone. I ran. Rode on the back of trucks, in buses; walked over fields and roads and mountains, In the cold and mud and rain; On a boat that leaked and almost sank and up a beach where babies lay face down in the sand. I ran until I couldn't run until I reached a row of huts and found a corner with a dirty blanket and a door that rattled in the wind. I came to a school. I looked through the window, they were learning all about volcanoes and drawing birds and singing. I went inside. My footsteps echoed the hall I pushed the door and faces turned towards me but the teacher didn't smile She said, there is no room

> for you, There is no chair for you to sit on, You have to go away. And then I understood that war had come here too.

The burgeoning of refugee numbers and the problems that they confront, has put a question mark over the legitimacy of the existing state system. The new states that have emerged as a result of decolonization have "inherited artificial boundaries, fragile national unity, brittle political systems and distorted economies". The nation-building experiments, which gave disproportionate advantage to the majority community and marginalized the minority groups, further worsened the overall situation. Mrs. Sadako Ogata, former United Nations High Commissioner for Refugees, has rightly highlighted the need to shift international attention "from the security of the borders to that of the people". Refugees are doubly insecure; "They flee because they are afraid, and in fleeing they start a precarious existence".

❐

2
Indian Experience: *Athithi Devo Bhava*

> I would leave one or two thoughts with you before I leave Colombo. Since you are earning your bread in this beautiful island, I would ask you to live as sugar in milk. Even as a cup of milk which is full to the brim does not overflow when sugar is gently added to it, the sugar accommodating itself in the milk and enriching its taste, in the same way I would like you to live in the island so as not to become interlopers and so as to enrich the lives of the people in whose midst you are living.
>
> **—Mahatma Gandhi**

The analogy of sugar and milk, which Gandhiji cited in his speech to the Indian community in Ceylon in November 1927, was in conformity not only with his personal convictions, but also with abiding Indian tradition of tolerance and goodwill. It made India a haven for immigrants and shelter-seekers from very early times.

A Haven of Immigrants

It is worth mentioning that St. Thomas brought Christianity to the Kerala coast, long before Vatican was Christianised. According to local oral history, St. Thomas came to Kodungallur in 52 AD and founded seven churches along the Kerala coast. The Syrian Christians, as they are called, successfully assimilated with the local people; they were Christian in faith, but in all else, they mingled with the environment in which they lived. They had a rightful place in society and shared common interests and took pride with the rest of citizens of Kerala that they were all Malayalees, speaking the same language, wearing the same clothes and following the same customs.

The Jews fleeing from Roman persecution also found refuge in Kodungallur in Kerala in 68 A.D. and from there, they moved to different parts of the country. There was a flourishing Jewish community in Cochin, until the Jews, after the Second World War, migrated to Israel. The Jews in Kerala lived, as one commentator has put it, "in the palpable absence of anti-Semitism, a cancer unknown in India" and, what is more, the Jewish community emerged in an environment, which for the most part "was hospitable, affectionate and nurturing".

It may be relevant to highlight the spirit of fraternity and equality which Guru Nanak, the founder of Sikhism, inculcated among his followers. Guru Nanak followed the principle of not giving an appointment to anybody who came to see him unless the visitor has partaken of food in the community kitchen (***langar***) – where Muslims, Christians, Brahmins and Shudras all sat together; this was a fine way of inculcating humility, equality and fraternity; and driving home the lesson that we are all children of the Eternal Master.

The Indian religious tolerance is well illustrated by an incident with reference to the arrival of the Parsis in India. As is well known, Parsis came to West Coast of India from Persia. They came with their sacred fire, fearing religious persecution from the Muslims. They went to the Kingdom of Navsari and requested the King to give them asylum. The King told them that the flourishing Muslim community in his State may not like the presence of Parsis in their midst. The Parsi religious leader requested the King to give him a glass of milk and some sugar. When the milk and sugar were brought, he put the sugar in the milk and gently stirred it. The milk did not overflow, but it became sweet. The Parsi religious leader informed the King that their presence in his kingdom would be like sugar in milk. It would only sweeten it, not spoil it. And it must be stated to the credit of the Parsis, a miniscule community in India today, numbering around 100,000 – they have contributed much to the economic, educational, cultural and industrial advancement of the country. And, what is more, they are proud to be regarded as an integral part of the Indian nation.

In the Indian tradition, a stranger who comes as a guest is referred to as *Athithi,* and the host is expected to treat him as God, next only to mother, father and teacher. In the *Yudha Kanda* of *Valmiki Ramayana,* when Vibhishana approached Rama for asylum, Rama told Sugriva, "O Sugriva, Chief of the Monkeys, please bring him here. I have granted him fearlessness, whether he is Vibhishana or Ravana".

Periya Puranam, the Tamil classic, mentions the story of the Chola King Meyyapurul Nayanar, who was not only a temporal King but also a "realized soul". One of his enemies wanted to kill him and came disguised as a devotee of Shiva. He greeted the King with folded hands that concealed a knife. When the King responded in the same way, his enemy stabbed and killed him. The King's aide, Duttan, wanted to catch the culprit, but the dying king dissuaded him, saying that the killer was a devotee of Shiva and should be treated as God himself. The King implored in soft tones, "Just ensure that the devotee of our Lord goes back safe to his place, unmolested by anyone". In other words the King saw divinity in every human being, particularly in the guest.

Thirukural, which had influenced and continues to influence the lives of the people in Tamil Nadu for several centuries, specifically mentions how those who come in search of food and succour should be treated. A few quotations from ***Thirukural*** are given below:

- All the household articles that one possesses at home are only for the sake of pleasing and making the guests happy.
- Even if it is nectar of the Gods, it should not be eaten alone by the householder, but should be shared with the guests.
- The life of the householder will not be spoiled by poverty, nor would his wealth go to waste, if he receives and feasts his guests.
- Lakshmi, the Goddess of Wealth, will live in the home of a person who treats his guests with a smiling face.
- A person who waits on his guests at home and looks forward to unexpected guests is Guest to the Gods.
- The quality of the hospitality cannot be measured. It depends upon the worth of the feast that is given.
- Just as the *Anchikam* flower fades when it is smelt, so also the guest is displeased when the host has an expression of displeasure on his face.

Silappadikaram, the great Tamil classic written by Ilango Adigal, describes in vivid detail how a person entrusted to another's care should be treated. Kuvundi tells

Madhavi how Kannaki should be taken care of: "When the merchants of the city discover who the father-in-law of the girl is, they will invite her and her husband into their well-guarded homes, considering it a privilege. Until we can bring her to these wealthy mansions, keep Kannaki under your protection. Give her a good cool bath and put black collirium on her long, reddened eyes. Rearrange her hair with fresh flowers. Dress her in well-washed garments, as is proper for people of her rank. Be her servant, she is of high birth, but be also her mother and guardian. Take care of her".

Movement of Refugees

In more recent times, the movement of refugees and displaced persons has seriously affected India and other South Asian countries. Nearly 20 million people crossed India-Pakistan borders before and after Indian independence. 10 million East Pakistani refugees came to India before the liberation of Bangladesh and 3.5 million Afghan refugees moved into Pakistan following the Soviet military intervention. Nearly 80,000 Tibetan refugees came to India after 1959 and were camped in different parts of the country. About 50,000 Chakmas had crossed over to Tripura, Arunachal Pradesh and other Northeastern States. India also provided shelter to 15,000 Afghan refugees and a few hundred ethnic Nepalese from Bhutan. A small number of Burmese students, fearing persecution from the military regime, have also been given asylum. There is a miniscule number of Iranians and Somalians in India. If we add Sri Lankan Tamil refugees to this figure, the total number of refugees and displaced persons looked after by India after independence would be approximately 25 million, which is more than the combined population of Sri Lanka, Singapore, Bhutan and Maldives.

Refugee Population in India

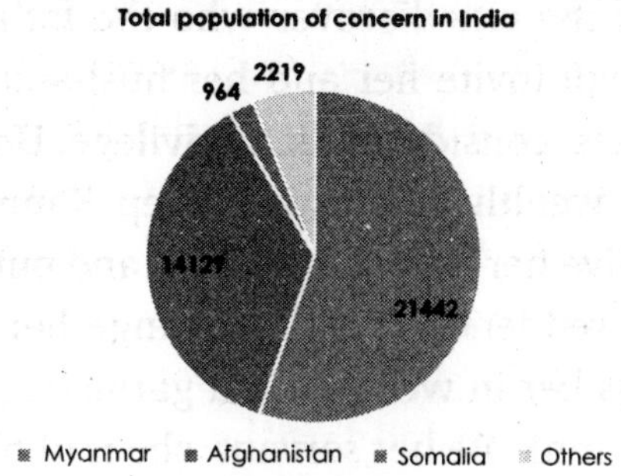

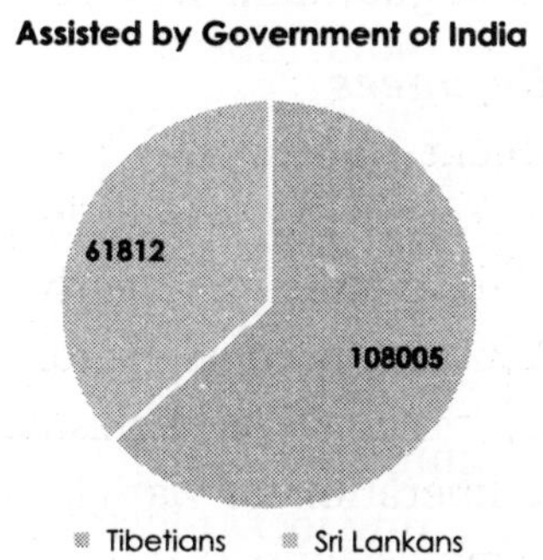

Source:http://www.unhcr.org/statistics/unhcrstats/5aaa4fd27/midyear-trends-june-2017.html
https://data2.unhcr.org/en/situations/myanmar_refugees

Refugee Population in South Asian Countries (Other than India)

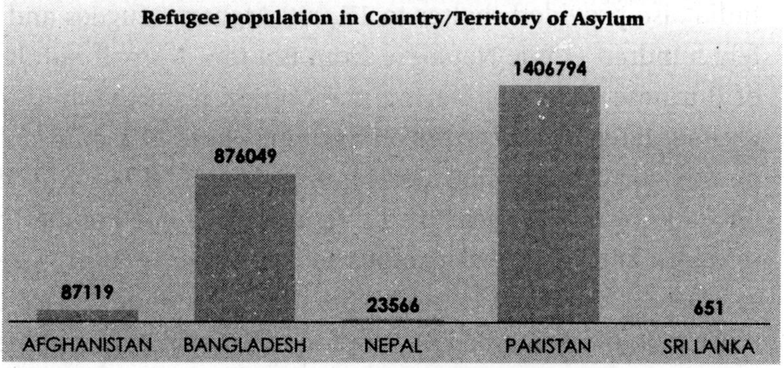

Source:http://www.unhcr.org/statistics/unhcrstats/5aaa4fd27/mid-year-trends-june-2017.html

All South Asian countries have been receiving and generating refugees. However, India has always been at the receiving end. Myron Weiner draws attention to two complex factors which have a bearing on the situation. All South Asian countries grant freedom of exit to their citizens, but none of them allow freedom of entry. Second, South Asian countries are unable to exercise effective control over their international borders. As a result, population movements in South Asia have consisted largely "of rejected peoples and unwanted migrants". Two illustrations are given below. In the northeastern states of India, especially in Assam, Tripura and Arunachal Pradesh, demographic changes are taking place as a result of outside influx, leading to increased tensions between the local people and immigrant population. In Sind, Pakistan, there is increasing antagonism towards ***Mujahirs***, who migrated after partition and played a prominent role in Karachi. Successful migrants are viewed with suspicion by local people, accentuating local tensions.

It has been estimated that since 1947, 35 to 40 million people have moved across inter-state boundaries in South Asia as displaced persons and refugees. This involuntary movement of people, according to Kamal Hussain, can be broadly described as "human rights violations...and ethnic intolerance, reinforced by high levels of poverty, landlessness and unemployment".

Location Aggravates the Problem

The geographic location of India, at the centre of South Asia, has also had its inevitable impact on the refugee situation. The island status of Sri Lanka and the archipelagic nature of Maldives have kept refugees away. The mountainous nature of Bhutan has deterred refugees. A majority of refugees in Pakistan and Bangladesh is from outside South

Asia – Afghans in the case of Pakistan and Rohingyas from Myanmar in the case of Bangladesh. As the only country that is contiguous to other South Asian countries, India has had to bear the brunt of refugees from within the region.

A few illustrations are given below to draw attention to the complex problems in South Asia. The creation of Pakistan precipitated large scale Hindu-Muslim and Sikh-Muslim clashes resulting, perhaps, in the "largest international flow of refugees in world history". In neighbouring Myanmar, attempts to "Burmanise" public services, introduction of land reforms and nationalization of retail trade compelled Indians to return to India. The Sri Lankan Government excluded a vast majority of Indian Tamils from citizenship by enacting discriminatory citizenship provisions. Colombo's assumption was that that those who did not qualify for Sri Lankan citizenship were Indian nationals.

What is more, the politics of "affirmative action" pursued by successive Sinhalese-dominated governments led to the exodus of large number of Sri Lankan Tamils to different parts of the world. The exacerbation of ethnic conflict and attempts to impose a military solution to the ethnic problem converted many Sri Lankan Tamils into refugees. When Bangladesh became independent, it faced the problems of "Bihari refugees" (Urdu-speaking Muslims). From late 1980s, the Rohingyas of Myanmar started pouring into Bangladesh. The Chakmas, the indigenous Buddhist tribe of the Chittagong hill tracts, moved into Tripura, Mizoram and Arunachal Pradesh as refugees.

The category of political refugees is a consequence of adverse political developments. They consist of Tibetans, who fled from Tibet to India; the East Pakistanis, who came to India following the military crackdown and the ensuing civil war; and the Afghans, who sought refuge in Pakistan following the anti-communist *coup* in Kabul. A different category comprises the illegal Bangladeshis in Assam (and to a lesser extent in other states), and the Nepalese in Bhutan. Though legally sanctioned, the movement of Nepalese into India and Indians into Nepal have created serious fissures in bilateral relations.

Offshoots of Conflict

Refugees are offshoots of conflicts and the resultant feeling of insecurity. The refugee, as Valentine Daniel, points out "mistrusts and is mistrusted. In a profound sense, he becomes a refugee even before fleeing the country in which one lives and continues to be a refugee even after one receives asylum in a new place among new people". The dynamics of the refugee problem is determined by "foreign" and "domestic" politics. What is more, in the South Asian situation, where geographical boundaries do not conform to ethnic affinities, ethnic brethren in the mother country champion the refugee cause. The presence of armed militants among the refugees and the acts of violence perpetrated by them has created problems of security in the host countries. For example, the abundant supply of arms available to the Afghan refugees, coupled with their involvement in the narcotics trade, has transformed the socio-economic-security profile of Pakistan. Similarly, when the host countries feel threatened numerically and economically by the refugees, they provide fertile soil for agitational politics. Assam is an example.

The forced migration in South Asia, as Prof. Mahendra Lama has pointed out, is of three types. First, the main villain is the State. By promoting policies of cultural homogeneity and upholding the interests of one community, the State makes it impossible for the minority groups to co-exist with the majority community. Second, a few South Asian Governments have resorted to forced eviction as a means of dealing with political dissidents. By denying citizenship to overwhelming Nepalese in Bhutan and by driving them out of the mountain kingdom, the Government has been able to concentrate power in the hands of a coterie in the royal palace. Third, whether it is Afghan refugees in Pakistan, East Pakistani refugees in India or Sri Lankan Tamil refugees in Tamil Nadu, the refugee phenomenon has become intertwined with the larger foreign policy objectives.

South Asian countries are signatories to major international humanitarian and human rights covenants. Three countries–India, Pakistan and Bangladesh–are members of the governing body of the UNHCR. What is more interesting, important leaders like M.A. Jinnah, Z.A. Bhutto, Pervez Musharraf, I.K. Gujral, L.K. Advani, Manmohan Singh and Ram Jethmalani were one-time refugees. Despite these plus points, none of the South Asian countries is a signatory to the 1951 U.N. Convention on Refugees, nor has any ratified the 1967 Protocol. South Asian countries have also not enacted any separate refugee legislation. As a result, the problems confronting the refugees are dealt with on an *ad hoc* basis.

However, there is one silver lining in the overall situation. The UNHCR in India has taken the initiative to sensitise the intelligentsia about the problems of refugees in South Asian countries. A number of seminars and workshops have been arranged in collaboration with Universities and organizations like the South Asian Association for Regional Cooperation in Law (SAARCLAW)and Indian Centre for Humanitarian Law and Research (ICHLR). Informal consultations have also taken place and a model law on the refugees has been drafted by the Indian Group of Concerned Eminent Persons, under the Chairmanship of Justice P.N. Bhagwati, former Chief Justice of India. Justice Bhagwati has succinctly posed the question facing South Asian countries as follows: "Would the setting up of an appropriate legal structure or framework not help to provide a measure of certainty in the States dealing with the problem of refugees, and provide greater protection to refugees?" India and other South Asian countries should seriously ponder over this question.

Moment of Glory

The suicide squad of the Liberation Tigers of Tamil Eelam (LTTE) assassinated Rajiv Gandhi on May 21, 1991. The Government and people of Tamil Nadu underwent a catharsis from which they are yet to recover. In a moment of agony and bitterness, the property and offices of the Dravida Munnetra Kazhagam (DMK) were vandalized by an angry mob. But it goes to the credit of the Tamil people that not even one single Sri Lankan Tamil refugee was harmed. It was a moment to be cherished, an illustration of tolerance and goodwill.

❐

3
Island in Distress

In his book, *Ceylon: Dilemmas of A New Nation,* Howard Wiggins dealt with group attitudes in the island. He referred to a study made by T.L. Green, formerly of the University of Ceylon. Seventy Sinhalese children were asked to characterize themselves and the Tamils. Sinhalese self-perception included terms like "kind, clever, rich, brave, jealous, proud, good, religious, courageous, lazy and honest". Their characterization of the Tamils was equally interesting: "cruel, clever, poor, diligent, cunning, rich, thrifty, ugly, arrogant, business minded and proud". Not even one Sinhala student attributed "bravery" as a quality of the Tamils!

How times have changed! *Serendib* (Arab name for Ceylon, which means the island of happy fortune), by early 1990s, had become one of the most notorious killing fields of the world. Torn by internal dissensions, Sri Lanka had become a fractured island. The "docile" Tamils had taken to the cult of the bomb and the bullet and those who supported the Liberation Tigers of Tamil Eelam (LTTE) were convinced that only a separate state would provide security and safety to the Tamils. But violence in Sri Lanka was not confined to Tamil areas alone. During 1988-90, aptly characterized as *Bhisana Samaya* (massive repression), Kelaniya Ganga and Kalu Ganga, Sri Lankan rivers of exquisite beauty, "were clogged with dead bodies and foamed with blood". And violence in Sri Lanka was no longer inter-ethnic, but intra-ethnic, with Tamils killing Tamils and Sinhalese killing Sinhalese, with the Sri Lankan State killing both, Sinhalese and Tamils. Bishop Reginald Heber, with prophetic vision, wrote in the nineteenth century:

> What though the spicy breezes blow
> soft over Ceylon's isle though every
> prospect pleases and only man is vile.

JVP Revolts

It is necessary to highlight the fact that the first major challenge to the Sri Lankan political system did not come from the Tamils, but from the Sinhalese. In April 1971, the Janatha Vimukti Peramuna (JVP), reflecting the disenchantment and frustration of the Sinhalese educated and under-privileged youth, raised the banner of armed revolt. This revolt of the youth was the first instance of "tensions between generations breaking out into military conflict on a national scale. The creed of generational war was linked to eradicating the colonial status which had ended two decades previously, but was presumed to be still in existence". The revolt was crushed with external assistance, but had far-reaching repercussions, as far as Sri Lankan political system was concerned. A State of Emergency was proclaimed in April 1971, which continued until February 1977. Thousands of Sinhalese youth were detained without trial. The armed forces had their first major experience in tackling a violent revolt.

Sri Lankan Governments could not find a lasting solution to the increasing dichotomy between the revolution of rising expectations of the youth and the outmoded system of education with stagnating economic opportunities. After remaining dormant for a few years, the JVP rose like a phoenix following the India-Sri Lanka Accord of 1987. The JVP leaders realized that they could spread their influence far and wide, if they could successfully mobilise anti-Indian sentiments. The Party, therefore, shifted its slogan from "socialism through class struggle" to "liberation through patriotic struggle". Capitalising on the Sinhala backlash, the JVP became the champion of Sinhala extremism, spread its own brand of violence, and following the dictum of "punishing the traitors", systematically annihilated political opponents. As a Sri Lankan writer has put it, the period saw the "Ruhuna (rightly or wrongly) once more rising to its traditional role as the "protector" of the Sinhala-Buddhist identity". For a few months, there were doubts regarding Colombo's capacity to tackle the deepening political crisis. Due to a variety of reasons, the JVP could not accomplish its objectives; the army gradually got the upper hand and systematically decimated Sinhalese youth.

After the killing of the JVP leader Rohana Wijeweera, Ranjan Wijeratne, then Defence Minister, boasted that the "match is over". Perhaps, from a long-term perspective, it is too early to write the obituary of the JVP. Today, the JVP has taken to the parliamentary path and, having enjoyed power, is getting more and more domesticated. Its revolutionary morale has got weakened. However, unless the basic problems confronting the Sinhalese youth – chauvinist traditions going back to the Dutugemunu period, combined with severe economic hardships – are not resolved, the reservoir from which the revolutionary youth derived its inspiration and strength will remain intact. In other words, the Sinhalese society is bound to live in social and political ferment for years to come.

It is interesting to note that a few JVP leaders and Tamil militants established contacts in jails, where they were detained by the Sri Lanka Freedom Party (SLFP) Government. Certain parallel features of the two movements need mention. The Tamil militants and JVP represented generational revolts, they revolted against the *status quo* politics of the Tamil United Liberation Front (TULF), led by the Vellallas and the UNP-SLFP politics led by the Goigamas. Prabhakaran was born in the Karaya caste and Wijeweera belonged to the Karavas. The two groups also subscribed to the path of armed struggle. The JVP at present is following the parliamentary path and the Tigers have been annihilated. But the grievances – social, economic and political – remain. How these frustrations and disenchantment will be mobilized by political forces need to be carefully watched.

Dynamics of Ethnic Politics

Sri Lanka is a fascinating laboratory for studying the dynamics of inter-ethnic relations. From a South Asian perspective, it is interesting to note that, in the era of de-colonisation, Ceylon was referred to as a "model colony". The transition to independence was smooth; there was no prolonged and bitter anti-colonial struggle as in India, Indonesia and Vietnam. On the eve of independence, it was a relatively peaceful country compared to the orgy of violence, that accompanied the birth of its northern neighbours, India and Pakistan. D.S. Senanayake, the first Prime Minister, was not only the leader of the majority Sinhalese community, but also had the tacit support of other minority groups. Most commentators felt that the newborn state would be politically stable and that the major ethnic groups would be integrated into one nation. The State was also committed to the ideals of democracy and promotion of social justice through welfare programmers.

Seventy years later, the political system had undergone a fundamental transformation. The common links and aspirations which united the elite among the Sinhalese and the Tamils have disappeared and Sri Lanka, in the 1990's, became one of the most notorious killing fields of the world. Though the war against the Tigers has been won, it has not led to ethnic reconciliation. What former President Chandrika Kumaratunga underlined a few years ago, still remains true. To quote Chandrika:

> We have failed to forge together the diverse communities of our peoples into one coherent and strong nation. We have faltered along for fifty years, permitting the differences to emerge and dominate our social fabric, rather than nurture the commonalities.

Two important strands in the Sri Lankan political fabric should be highlighted. During the 1950s and 1960s, Sri Lanka was undoubtedly the most vibrant democracy in Asia. The governments changed at regular intervals, through free and fair elections. All the essentials of a dynamic democracy – free press, independence of the judiciary, rule of law, free and fair polls, strong trade unions and active students unions - were in existence. All these welcome features were soon subjected to severe stresses and strains. Mrs. Sirimavo Bandaranaike promulgated an Emergency following the outbreak of the JVP revolt in April 1971, which continued up to 1977. Northern and eastern parts of the country were under spells of emergency till the end of the war in 2009. Constitutions were tampered with and democratic institutions were subverted. Political assassinations became common and militant groups, especially the Tigers, were armed to the teeth. Chandrika Kumaratunga and the People's Alliance which came to power in 1994 on the slogan of peace and stability, could not deliver the promise due to the intransigence of the Tigers. War resumed with attendant horror tactics on both sides. The Presidential election of December 2009 was held against the backdrop of an abortive attempt to assassinate the President. During the last stages of the ethnic conflict, war against the Tigers degenerated into a war against Tamils and nearly 40,000 innocent Tamils were killed. The promised 'new dawn' did not materialize after the end of war, and the political scene today is characterized by a bitter struggle to mobilise the majority community on the basis of competitive communal politics.

Equally noteworthy was the high PQLI – Physical Quality of Life Index – which made Sri Lanka envy of the Third World countries. Successive governments – SLFP and UNP – invested considerable proportion of the national wealth on education, health and infra-structure. As a result, the quality of life in Sri Lanka was favourably compared with developed Scandinavian countries. However, the fuelling of the war machine resulted in diversion of funds to defence. Even so, Sri Lanka still ranks high in South Asia in terms of human development index.

Falsification of History

To look at the past through the prism of the present can lead to falsification of history. The projection of Sinhalese and Tamils as two antagonistic entities at war with each another for several centuries by Sinhalese/Tamil writers is an illustration of the well-known axiom that truth and objectivity are the first casualties in times of conflict. As Eric

Hobsbawm has pointed out, "History is the raw material for nationalist or ethnic or fundamentalist ideologies, as poppies are the raw material for heroin addiction". Stanley Tambiah, after years of painstaking research, has come to the conclusion that Sinhalese and Tamils share many parallel features of "traditional caste, kinship, popular religious cult, customs and so on. But they have come to be divided by their mythic characters and tendentious historical understandings of the past". He has also exploded the myth that the Sinhalese are fair Aryans and the Tamils are dark Dravidians. Quoting Gananath Obeysekere, Tambiah adds, "if it were possible to trace the present day Sinhalese population's ancestry far enough, all lines in major part would lead to South India". According to Obeysekere, "Biologically speaking, those whom we call Sinhala are in fact racially inter-mixed with South Indian peoples and with aboriginal groups like the Veddas, and the Tamils who live in the north and the east, are also similarly biologically mixed".

In his monumental study of the ***People of India,*** K. Suresh Singh has remarked that several communities can be classified as having more than one religion. It is interesting to note that Sinhalese religious practices also point to the same direction. The Hindu Bhakti cult has influenced Theravada Buddhism and there are images of Hindu Gods in Buddhist temples. The deity of Skanda (Muruga) in Kataragama, located near the Yala Sanctuary in the southeast of the island, continues to be the "major institutional intersection of several religious faiths. Hindus, Buddhists, Christians and Moslems – all go to Kataragama where the atmosphere is one of tolerance and goodwill". During my visit to the temple, I found Buddhist pilgrims far outnumbering the Hindus. The Sinhalese carry the ***Kavadi*** with great devotion and fervour.

According to ***Mahavamsa,*** the Buddhist sacred text, the founding father of the first Sinhala kingdom was Prince Vijaya, a prince from North India, who came to Sri Lanka with 700 followers and decided to settle in the island. They did not have any women with them and, therefore, they brought women from the Pandyan kingdom in Tamil Nadu. Vijaya himself married the Pandyan King's daughter. In other words, even according to Buddhist texts, from the very beginning, the Sinhala nation was a product of assimilation between the Sinhalese and the Tamils.

Few Sri Lankan scholars want to subscribe to the objective truth that Buddhism was a virile religion in South India from the first century to the seventh century A.D. and the spread and efflorescence of Theravada form of Buddhism during the Anuradhapura and Pollanaruwa periods, had much to do with their contacts with Buddhist centers of learning in South India. Recent research in linguistics also reveals several commonalities. According to Gunawardene, "in grammatical structure, Sinhalese was Dravidian (i.e. South Indian), though the vocabulary was mainly Aryan (North Indian)".

Despite cultural commonalities, the chauvinists among the Sinhalese and the Tamils propagate the falsehood of age-old animosities between the two communities. Their tendentious arguments remind us of the famous statement of Voltaire, "If you believe in absurdities, you will commit atrocities". It is my submission that the Sinhalese-Tamil conflict is a product of the post-independence politics, an offshoot of the nation-building experiment, where the Sinhalese leaders wanted to build the nation on the basis of the Sinhalese language and Buddhist religion to the exclusion of minority claims, and, on the other, to the politics of ethnic mobilization resorted to by chauvinist Sinhalese and Tamil leaders.

What is of relevance, however, for our analysis, is the subjective belief of the Sinhalese and the Tamils that they are unique and separate communities. And, as Gananath Obeysekere points out, in crucial moments of ethnic identity formation, the "identity is influenced more by myths of the past than actual occurrences".

Competing Nationalist Narratives

An analysis of the ideological constructs and a review of significant Sinhalese writings provide fascinating insights into the majority community's concept of nation-building, which had been the main stumbling block to the emergence of a tolerant multi-ethnic society in Sri Lanka. The concept of *Sinha Dvipa* (island of the Sinhalese) and *Dhamma Dvipa* (island of the Buddhist Dharma) were exploited to portray the Tamils and the Moslems as non-native intruders, who had to be subordinate to the "sons of the soil". The popular Sinhalese formulation was that the Sinhalese have only Sri Lanka, while the Tamils can go back to India and the Muslims to Arabia.

The educational system also helped to perpetuate these dangerous myths. The Council of Communal Harmony, which undertook a study of the Sinhalese and Tamil textbooks, came to the following conclusion: "While the Tamil books "do seek to create an understanding of and respect for the way of life and culture of non-Tamil and non-Hindu linguistic and religious groups, and do attempt to project a sense of common national identity, the Sinhala books are exclusively monocultural in their content i.e. the way of life they present is not only solely Sinhala, but also solely Sinhala-Buddhist. The Tamils are identified throughout the book as traditional adversary..."

The nationalist narrative authored by President Jayewardene is also replete with such falsehoods. *Golden Threads* was published in May 1984 by the Sri Lankan Government. The book claims to be a "sketch of the story of the island" and is dedicated "to the youth of Sri Lanka ...to whom the torch must pass". Sankaran Krishna has pointed out, the text begins by locating "the narrator and his audience, the narrator is someone who has, in an Olympian metaphor, led the charge, carried the torch of the national journey and is preparing to bestow the responsibility on his young wards".

Jayewardene's view of Sri Lankan history should be highlighted because it throws light on the man and his mission. The book is divided into three parts: First, it deals with post-544 BC to 1815 AD. According to *Mahavamsa,* Prince Vijaya came to the island in 544 BC and the Kandyan kings surrendered their sovereignty to the British in 1815 AD. By beginning Sri Lanka's history with the arrival of Prince Vijaya, Jayewardene completely blocks out the earlier rich history of the country; he also "pushes to the margins the Tamils and other ethnic and religious communities, who have no comparable mythic charter of their presence". Nor does Jayewardene consider 1948, the year in which Sri Lanka became independent, as a landmark. More interesting, the third part begins with the UNP coming to power and Jayewardene becoming the Prime Minister in 1977.

Throughout the book, Sri Lanka and the Sinhala nation are used to convey the same idea. In a Seminar organised by the Centre for South and Southeast Asian Studies, University of Madras, a few years ago, Jayadeva Uyangoda made the telling comment that in the Sinhalese language, the term used for nation-building is *Jathiya Godanegama.* It means the making of the Sinhala nation and not the Sri Lankan nation. Jayewardene projects the Sri Lankan Tamils as intruders, who disturbed the peace and harmony of the country. The book records: "In the first quarter of the thirteenth century from South India came the *Magha* – the Tiger. The wasteland that he created became the kingdom of the malaria, the domain of the anopheles, breeding prodigiously in the dark stagnant waters of the great irrigation works".

Jayewardene did not display even an iota of sympathy for the minority groups, who became victims of communal riots at regular intervals in the post-independence era. He referred to terrorism – "A world phenomenon raised its ugly head in the north and the east and some Tamils joined them to press for separation. In 1980, these activities increased and the killing of the Sinhala security forces in the north in 1983 was followed by Sinhala-Tamil riots throughout the island". By equating the Tamil grievances and resultant violence with terrorism, Jayewardene clearly proved that he was not a neutral, non-sectarian Head of State. When the communal holocaust took place in July 1983 – a "dark night of the collective soul" as Jonathan Spencer rightly puts it – Jayewardene not only failed to express any sympathy for the victims, but also failed to condemn the lumpen sections of Sinhalese population, which ran amok in the Tamil areas of Colombo. As Paul Sieghart, the distinguished Jurist, remarked:

> The President did not see it fit to utter one single word in sympathy for the victims of violence and the destruction, which he lamented. If his concern was to establish communal harmony in the island, whose national unity he was so anxious to preserve by law, it was a misjudgment of monumental proportions.

The communal riots and the resultant trauma were the major factors that triggered the refugee phenomenon. Within Colombo alone, nearly 100,000 Tamils, more than half the total Tamil population in the city, were displaced. There was hardly any Tamil family that escaped death, destruction and displacement. A Tamil woman, who was a victim of repeated cycles of violence, exclaimed: "To be a Tamil is to live in fear". The agony and anguish of the Tamil population was expressed by R.R. Sivalingam, the Indian Tamil political activist, as follows:

> The Tamils of Sri Lanka are in anguish. We are watching ourselves. Is it a crime to be a Tamil in this country? Our expectations have all been shattered. Generations of effort to build a base of life have all been shattered to smithereens in a matter of few hours. How long? Oh! How long will it take for us to feel as brothers and sons of the soil?

The Sinhalese – majority community with a minority complex – were consistently opposed to devolution and federalism. They believed that federalism would be the first step towards the creation of a separate State. The three Constitutions and their underlying ideologies contributed to the exacerbation of the ethnic conflict, the distortion of liberal democracy and the emergence of authoritarianism. The first Constitution of Sri Lanka, the Soulbury Constitution of 1947, promulgated by Britain one year before independence, enshrined majoritarian democracy in a unitary state. Provision was made for the protection of minority rights, under Section 29 (2) of the Constitution, which prescribed limitations on legislative sovereignty. The 1972 Constitution marked a distinct departure from the past. The United Front

Government, led by Mrs. Sirimavo Bandaranaike, equated the overwhelming majority with national consensus. The Tamil demand for federalism and protection of minority rights were ignored. On the other hand, the Constitution gave Buddhism an elevated position within the country and made Sinhala the official language. The role of the judiciary was eroded. As Dr. Radhika Coomaraswamy pointed out, "Not one case on fundamental rights was decided by the Courts during the tenure of the Constitution".

The Second Republican Constitution of 1978 introduced the system of Executive Presidency. The main objective of the Constitution makers was to provide political stability with a strong executive head, free from the whims and fancies of Parliament. The "mighty executive" coupled with "devalued parliament" hastened the downfall of democracy and paved the way for authoritarianism. A free press and regular elections became memories of the past. Concentration of power through parliament, as in the 1972 Constitution or through the President as in the 1978 Constitution, did not contribute to political stability. The period witnessed two JVP uprisings and also intensification of ethnic conflict. As Regi Siriwardena aptly put it, "centralisation begot not order, but disorder".

The India-Sri Lanka Accord of 1987 and the Thirteenth Amendment to the Constitution were significant steps in the introduction of devolution of powers. In sum, the 13th Amendment aimed at sharing of powers between the majority and minority communities and between the Centre and the Provincial Councils. Unfortunately, in the perception of a large number of Sinhalese, the whole exercise was seen as an imposition by India. While one section of the Government, led by President Jayewardene and Gamini

Dissanayake, supported the Accord, an equally powerful section, led by Prime Minister Premadasa and National Security Minister Lalith Athulathmudali, tried to sabotage it. Without a national consensus and Tamil participation, the Accord itself became a source of discord in Sri Lanka.

Given the Sinhalese ideology, which subscribes to centralisation of state power and close identification of the nation state with the Sinhalese community, it was inevitable that the Provincial Council system got mired in serious difficulties. The Provincial Council of the Northeast had only a short life of nineteen months - November 1988 to May 1990. It lacked financial resources and, through some disingenuous mechanisms, central dominance was reestablished in many areas like agriculture and transport, which were devolved subjects. In the inaugural address to the India-Sri Lanka Consultation on Devolution, Prof. G.L. Peries admitted: "In fact, we have no devolution at all, decentralisation yes, devolution, no".

Sri Lankan Politics – An Overview

The early Tamil nationalists like Ponnambalam Ramanathan and G.G. Ponnambalam viewed Ceylon as a single political unit transcending ethnic, religious, and linguistic differences. Their successors got disillusioned with the political system, with the passage of the Sinhala Only Act of 1956. Further, the irreconcilable perceptions of injustice and relative deprivation by Sri Lankan Tamils and the Sinhalese – the former being an "achieving minority" and the latter being a majority community which felt "historically deprived" – further widened the chasm between the two.

I would like to submit two propositions which can be considered as the yardstick for the success of nation-building experiments in multi-ethnic societies in South Asia. First, the political system should provide sufficient space for minorities so that they can preserve, promote and foster their identities, while being a part of the united country. Second, a federal polity with entrenched provisions for sharing powers between the Centre and the States, can lead to softening of secessionist demands and pave the way for eventual political integration. Two illustrations, one a success story from India and second, a tragic narrative from Sri Lanka, both relating to Tamil minority groups, are given below. What is interesting to note are the differing political developments and contrasting responses to the issue of nation building.

In Sri Lanka, the Tamil political leaders drifted from collaboration with the Sinhalese elite and eventually began to demand a separate state of Tamil Elam. The Dravidian movement in India followed a diametrically opposite course. The scholars studying the Dravidian movement are unanimous in pointing out the important milestones – the formation of the Justice Party and the non-Brahmin movement from 1917 of E.V. Ramaswamy Naicker's Self Respect Movement and anti-Hindi agitation, the formation of the *Dravida Kazhagam* in the mid-1940s and its advocacy of a separate state of *Dravida Nadu*, the formation of the Dravida Munnetra Kazhagam (DMK) under C.N. Annadurai in 1949; the coming into power of the DMK following the 1967 general election; and the domination of the DMK and its offshoot Anna Dravida Munnetra Kazhagam (AIAMK), formed in 1972 in the politics of Tamil Nadu. The DMK gradually got "domesticated" because the Indian political system provided sufficient political space within which the Tamil identity and regional autonomy could be protected and fostered. What is more, the domestication of the DMK was evident even before Annadurai formally renounced secessionism in 1962 (after the Sino-Indian conflict) and the 16th Amendment to the Constitution (which proscribed secessionism and required from all candidates, seeking political office, an oath of upholding the Constitution) was passed. The DMK/AIADMK stakes in the unity of India got further strengthened when these parties started sharing power with the Centre. The AIADMK joined the Charan Singh Government in the 1970s and the DMK joined the V.P. Singh Government in the 1980s.

In contrast, an overview of Sri Lankan Tamil politics since independence clearly shows that the Tamils had been mainly "reactive" to Sinhalese politics. Since Sinhalese-dominated Governments never fulfilled their hopes and aspirations, frustrations became intense; demands more radical, which finally culminated with the demand for a separate state of Tamil Eelam in Vaddukoddai in 1976. The politics of Tamil opposition started with the demand for balanced representation and responsive co-operation, which spanned the period from 1948 to 1956; the demand progressed to federal state and non-cooperation during 1967-1972; escalated to separatist slogans during 1973-1976; and ended with the demand for a separate state in 1976. But while the demands changed, the mainstream Tamil political leadership confined themselves to strategies of peaceful agitation, parliamentary and non-parliamentary alike. From 1979, militancy began to creep into Tamil politics. To the Tamil youth, majoritarian democracy meant the rule of brute Sinhala majority. They were also not enamoured with earlier forms of peaceful struggle.

By mid-1970s, the Sri Lankan Tamils, who were, to begin with, "reluctant secessionists" began to define themselves as a separate nation, entitled to self-determination and a separate state. Discriminatory legislative enactments and governmental policies in the areas of language, education, land colonization, religion and employment opportunities; the abrogation of the Bandaranaike-Chelvanayagam Pact of 1956 and Senanayake-Chelvanayagam Pact of 1965, which conferred limited autonomy to the Tamil areas; and, above all, brutal military repression, all convinced the Tamils that their legitimate rights could be guaranteed only by a separate State.

Tamils – No Unity

It is necessary to highlight the fact that, despite their adherence to a common language, the Tamils of Sri Lanka are not a homogenous group. The Sri Lankan Tamils are sub-divided into three categories: the Jaffna Tamils, the Batticaloa Tamils and the Colombo Tamils. The Jaffna Tamil society is dominated by the Vellalas, and in the eastern region, by the Mukkuvars. There are also differences in kinship – the Jaffna kinship is traced bilaterally, while, in the eastern region, the matrilineal system survives. Jaffna from the early 1980s was in a state of social ferment; the sidelining of the Tamil United Liberation Front (T.U.L.F.) not only implied the fading away of the moderates, but also sounded the death knell of Vellala domination of Tamil politics. The ethnic conflict was, in many ways, a leveler of Tamil society, which explained how Prabhakaran, belonging to the fisherman-merchant community of *Karaiyar,* could become the leader of the major Tamil militant group. Support to the Tamil militancy was less in the east, where the Tamils have co-existed with the Sinhalese and the Moslems. Some eastern Tamils also expressed concern that, in a state dominated by the Jaffna Tamils, they would receive second class treatment. The largest concentration of Tamils today is in Colombo and its suburbs. Most of them work in government offices and in private firms: many others are professionals–doctors, engineers, lawyers, teachers and accountants. A few others are engaged in business. With law and order deteriorating in the North and the East, many Sri Lankan Tamils have moved to Colombo. Some of them consider the capital to be a 'transit camp' for eventual migration abroad. Despite their vulnerability, the Colombo Tamils have nothing to gain from a separate state. In fact, in 1994 most of them voted for the People's Alliance in the Parliamentary elections. Similarly, a majority of them voted for the UNP candidate Ranil Wickremesinghe in the Presidential election.

Mention should also be made of the Sri Lankan Tamil community settled abroad and its impact on the contemporary Sri Lankan scene. The Sri Lankan Tamils, like the Malayalees, had always been migratory. Many educated Tamils, during the British period, migrated to Malaya, Singapore, Australia, United States and England. In fact, the remittances of these people sustained Tamil society. Jaffna was popularly referred to as the "post office economy". From the 1960s, with diminution of employment opportunities, further aggravated by the blatant pro-Sinhalese polices of successive Governments, number of Sri Lankan academicians, doctors, engineers, scientists, accountants and other skilled personnel left the shores of Sri Lanka. From 1983, thousands of Sri Lankan Tamils left the island as refugees. Smarting under an acute sense of deprivation, the Sri Lankan Tamils abroad became the ardent supporters of the separate state of Tamil Eelam. They provided considerable financial and propaganda support to the Tigers. According to some estimates, the monthly contribution from the Tamil expatriates to the L.T.T.E. was US Dollars one million. What is more, they formed influential lobbies in Western capitals and helped in a big way in the internationalisation of the ethnic conflict. Mention should be made of Kandaswamy and the Tamil Information Centre in London which carried on successful lobbying with international human rights organisations like the Amnesty International and the Minority Rights Group. The Tamil cause suffered irreparable loss when Kandaswamy was assassinated by one of the militant groups for its own selfish ends.

The Indian Tamils, as Valentine Daniel points out, "are different from the Jaffna Tamils and the Sinhalese, they have also come to be different from the Tamils of the mainland", whom they left 150 years ago. They are the descendants of the Tamil labourers, who were brought to the island by the British colonialists to provide much-needed labour for the development of coffee, tea, rubber and coconut plantations. They formed the bulk of labour that turned the malaria-infested forests of Sri Lanka into smiling tea plantations that sustain the Sri Lankan economy even today.

Unfortunately after independence, the Indian Tamils were reduced to the status of a merchandise to be divided between the two countries in the name of good neighbourly relations. To the ruling elite in New Delhi and Colombo, they were an agonising and embarrassing set of statistics; for the estate management, docile cheap labour to be exploited to the hilt; for the fanatics among Sinhalese, the easiest and defenceless victims in times of communal conflict. By the Sirimavo-Shastri Pact of 1964 and Sirimavo-Indira Gandhi Pact of 1974, New Delhi agreed to confer citizenship on 6,00,000 plus their natural increase, whereas Colombo agreed to confer citizenship on 4,00,000 (plus their natural increase), on the ratio of 7:4.

It is the tragedy of India – Sri Lanka relations that these Agreements, which had a bearing on the lives of thousands of people of Indian origin, were finalised by the two Governments without taking into consideration the feelings and views of the Tamil plantation workers. From the Sinhalese perspective, it was a major victory; it repatriated many to India by giving citizenship to a few. S. Thondaman, leader of the Ceylon Workers Congress, aptly described the situation:

> We are a community of human beings, with soul, mind and body with personality and cannot be apportioned between countries like beasts of burden at other's whims and fancies, only to maintain good neighbourly relations. Humanity cannot be converted to merchandise in this modern age.

In his absorbing novel, *Refuge,* Gopal Gandhi movingly describes the inhuman conditions in which the plantation workers of Indian origin lived. When their applications for Sri Lankan citizenship were rejected, they did not know what to do. Avadai, a toothless old man, called by the fellow workers as the "wise one", echoed their feelings:

> We came to this land, because our own land could not sustain us… I remember how parched the earth was, how hungry we all were in our village of Avur in Pudukkottai. My father said, "Come let us go and register in the Ceylon office". And so we registered and came here. We came in order to be able to work, to eat…And now we have lost links with native land, when we have sent our roots deep into this soil like the

> tea bushes planted by us, we are told ... that we do not belong here, that we must go back to India, that if we stay of here, we will have no rights. Is this fair? Is this just?

Though the Indian Tamils share common bonds of ethnicity and language with the Sri Lankan Tamils, the problems that they face and the aspirations that they entertain are, in many ways, different from their counterparts in the northern and eastern parts of the island. Unlike the Sri Lankan settlements in the Jaffna peninsula, the plantations are surrounded by Sinhalese villages, which are located in the heartland of the Sinhalese people. This stark reality has made them realise that their present and future are closely intertwined with the Sinhalese and they must co-exist with the Sinhalese population. In other words, Tamil Elam, even if it comes through, would not lead to the political salvation of the Indian Tamils.

If the problem of statelessness, hanging like a Damocles' sword over Indian Tamils, was resolved amicably, it was mainly due to the astute and dynamic leadership of Thondaman. With a judicious mix of parliamentary and extra-parliamentary struggles, he was able to extract, from recalcitrant Sinhalese leaders, the prize of citizenship to his people. The legislative enactment of 2003 provided citizenship even to the residue of the Sirimavo-Shastri Pact, who had not yet been repatriated to India. But the basic question of their safety and security still remains. Though the Indian Tamils did not subscribe to the demand for Tamil Eelam and their representative organisation, the Ceylon Workers Congress, was part of the Government from 1978, the Indian Tamils are most vulnerable in times of communal conflict. The communal violence of 1977, 1981 and 1983 clearly demonstrated the utter helplessness of these people against lumpen sections of Sinhalese population.

Describing the communal riots that took place in the plantation areas, soon after Jayewardene came to power in 1977, Sivanandan has written:

> It was the plantation workers who suffered most. Their line rooms were burnt; their possessions looted, the men beaten, the women gang-raped. And they ended in transit camps. Transit to where, though? Jaffna? But Jaffna was not their own.

Attempts made by Tamil militant groups to co-opt the plantation youth into their movements did not make much headway. Except for isolated pockets, the Indian Tamils remained aloof from Sri Lankan Tamil militants. However, in the long run, the winds of change will cast their impact on the Indian Tamils also. In other words, the future of the Indian Tamil community and Sri Lankan Tamil – Indian Tamil relations will be determined by the manner in which the wider question of Sinhala-Tamil relations is settled.

Of equal importance is the changing profile of the Muslim community in Sri Lanka. They are scattered throughout the island, but there is a concentration of the Muslims in the east. The Muslim settlements can be traced back to the heydays of Arab maritime trade activities in the early medieval period. Confined initially to the coastal areas, they gradually spread to other parts of the country. The Muslims seek their identity, not in terms of language, but, in terms of religion. Most of them are traders though, in the eastern province, they are also engaged in agriculture and fishing. Most of them are bilingual, with equal proficiency in Sinhala and Tamil.

In the early years of independence, the leadership of the Muslim community came from the affluent trading classes. They looked to Colombo, and not to Jaffna, for political inspiration. Being pragmatic, they supported the two major Sinhalese parties, the UNP and the SLFP and reaped maximum dividends. The Muslims are against the idea of Tamil Eelam. If it comes about they would become a mini-minority within a minority. A divided country would endanger their very existence. In day-to-day activities, the community hardly co-operated with the Federal Party and its successor, the TULF. In the 1977 election, the TULF fielded a few Muslim candidates, but all of them were decisively defeated. Moreover, the UNP and the SLFP were vying with each another in wooing the Muslims.

As the ethnic conflict gathered momentum, the Muslims in the east began to assert themselves. In 1980, the Sri Lanka Muslim Congress (SLMC) was formed under the leadership of MHM Ashraff. The SLMC made its debut in Parliament in 1989 with four seats; in the 1994 elections, the SLMC allied with Chandrika Kumaratunga and won seven seats. Given the slender majority of the ruling party, minority support becomes crucial in Sri Lankan political system.

The emergence of the SLMC and its stout opposition to the demand for Tamil Eelam led to violent clashes between the Tigers and the Muslims. The creation of an armed civilian force, the Muslim Home Guard, further widened the schism between the two. In August 1990, the Tigers massacred 122 innocent Muslims, who were offering prayers in two mosques in Kattankudy village. Two weeks later, 164 Muslims were hacked to death. In April 1992, 75 Muslims were massacred in Alinchipothana village in Polonnaruwa district; six months later, nearly 250 Muslim men, women and children became victims of LTTE violence in Palliagoddalla village in the same district. In October 1990, the Tigers ordered the Muslims in the Jaffna peninsula to vacate their homes within 72 hours. Nearly 75,000 Muslims fled, leaving behind their property which was looted by the LTTE. The displaced Muslims took asylum in refugee camps in Puttalam, Anuradhapura and Kurunegala districts. In later years, Balasingham expressed regret and admitted that their policy against the Muslims was a mistake. The war has ended, the TNA has been voted to power in the Northern Province, but an overwhelming majority of Muslims still remain in the refugee camps outside Jaffna province.

The apparent prosperity of the Muslim community has created jealousy and suspicion among the majority Sinhalese community also. Anti-Muslim riots took place in Amparai and soon spread to Kandy in February-March 2018. Shops, properties and mosques were destroyed. The security forces intervened and the situation was brought under control. Though there is apparent calm, the tensions between the two communities still persist.

An unfortunate irony of the Sri Lankan situation must be highlighted. The Sri Lankan Tamils complain, and rightly so, that they were discriminated against by successive Sinhala-dominated governments. But what about the fate of the Muslims? Sandwiched between Sinhalese and Tamils, the Muslims were subjected to attacks by both Sinhalese and Tamils. The tragedy of Sri Lanka, as late Neelam Thiruchelvam has pointed out:

> ...the violence of the victim soon consumed the victim and the victim also became possessed by the demons of racial bigotry and intolerance which had characterized

> the oppressor. These are seen in the fratricidal violence between Tamils and Muslims, in the massacres at the Kattankudy mosque, in Welikanda and Medirigiya, and in the forcible expulsion of the Muslims from the Mannar and Jaffna districts.

War Ends, Ethnic Reconciliation still Elusive

The decimation of the LTTE in May 2009 is undoubtedly one of the most spectacular events in modern Sri Lankan history. The victory was remarkable because, not so long ago, Sri Lanka watchers were unanimous that neither side could impose its will over the other through military means and the only solution to the protracted ethnic conflict was for the two warring sides to come together and negotiate a political settlement based on a federal model.

The factors that led to the decline and fall of the Tigers, considered to be one of the most ruthless and, at the same time, highly motivated guerrilla organizations in the world, have been analysed elsewhere. While the military dimension of the estranged Tamil nationalism has come to an end, the problems of rehabilitation and economic reconstruction, along with ethnic reconciliation and nation-building still remain to be addressed by the ruling elite.

The war had been won, but the manner in which the military victory was accomplished continues to be a subject matter of great controversy. The final stages of the war witnessed gross violations of human rights on both sides. Suffering reverse after reverse, Prabhakaran began to forcibly recruit young boys and girls into the "baby brigade"; they were sent to the battlefield without proper training and naturally became cannon fodder in the conflict between the Lions and the Tigers. The Tigers used the civilian population as human shields and physically prevented and, at times, shot the Tamil civilians under their control, who were trying to escape from the battlefield. The situation degenerated to such an extent that the Tigers could not even put a semblance of effective retaliation against the monstrous onslaught of Sri Lanka's artillery and Multi Barrel Rocket Launcher (MBRL) barrage, that killed civilians and combatants alike. Domestic conflicts are generally between two unequal sides, because the resources that the State can mobilise are far in excess of its opponent. In the Sri Lankan case, by early 2008, the Tigers had virtually committed *hara kiri* by their wanton killing of political opponents, the many acts of terrorism leading to their proscription and international isolation, the revolt led by Karuna which led to the loss of the east, and above all, the naval blockade by the Sri Lankan Navy, leading to the disruption of the supply lines and the annihilation of the Sea Tigers. Finally, the hope that Prabhakaran entertained that international intervention would take place and compel Colombo to declare ceasefire turned out to be false. Determined to annihilate the Tigers, the Sri Lankan armed forces pursued their goal relentlessly. Finally, as M.R. Narayana Swamy has written: "Prabhakaran, who had become a legend, was finally killed in the same callous and brutal manner he had so often used to send so many thousands to their death".

Nine years are over since the war against the Tigers has ended; flushed with victory, the Sinhalese leaders are engaged in competitive one-upmanship. Ethnic reconciliation remains a distant dream. The lesson is clear to all students of contemporary history. If the political system does not provide for tolerance of multiple identities, tensions and fissures will soon develop. A meaningful solution to the problems of ethnicity and nation-building can be found only if the political system enshrines tolerance, devolution, power sharing and autonomy.

The greatness of a nation, Mahatma Gandhi said, depends upon how secure the minorities feel in that country. Twelve days before his assassination, Mahatma Gandhi wrote in the *Harijan:*

> All Hindus, Moslems, Sikhs, Parsees, Christians and Jews, who people the vast sub-continent and have adopted it as their motherland, have an equal right to it. No one has a right to say that it belongs to the majority community only and that the minority community can only remain there as an underdog.

❑

4
Island of Refugees

> My son is in Jaffna, wife in Colombo, father in the Wanni, mother, old and sick, in Tamil Nadu, relatives in Frankfurt, a sister in France and I, like a camel that has strayed in Alaska am stuck in Oslo. Are our families cotton pillows, to be torn and scattered by the monkey fate?
>
> **—V.I.S. Jayapalan**

A small country, with a population of 22.4 million, Sri Lanka is one of the world's principal sources of refugees and internally displaced persons. Nearly half of the 2.3 million strong Sri Lankan Tamil population have been rendered homeless and have migrated to different parts of the world or remain internally displaced. At the end of the Fourth Eelam War, according to UNHCR, there were 8,00,000 IDPs in "welfare centers" in Sri Lanka. Because of the "ethnic cleansing" pursued by the LTTE, when it was in control of the Northern Province, 90,000 Muslims were rendered homeless and they continue to live in camps in Puttalam and Anuradhapura. Though peace has returned to Sri Lanka, majority of Muslims have not yet returned to their homes. In an issue paper published in October 1991, the US

Committee on Refugees rightly characterised Sri Lanka as an "Island of Refugees".

Sri Lankans being displaced in their country is not a new phenomenon. In 1958, following the introduction of "Sinhala Only" Act and subsequent peaceful Satyagraha in the Galle Face Green, there were large-scale riots in Colombo; thousands of Tamils had to leave Colombo and other Sinhalese areas and move to the north and the east. In 1977, after the general elections, which returned UNP to power, communal clashes erupted in different parts of the island. A large number of Tamils had to take shelter in camps. In mid-1981, on the eve of the expiry of the Sirimavo - Shastri Pact, large-scale violence was unleashed in the plantation areas to drive away as many Indian Tamils as possible from the island.

Communal Holocaust, July 1983

The unprecedented July 1983 riots in Colombo were undoubtedly a turning point in modern Sri Lankan history. As the radical humanist writer A. Sivanandan wrote in the *Race and Class:* "There have been no race riots in Sri Lanka since independence ...What there has been is a series of increasingly virulent pogroms against the Tamil people by the Sinhala State – resulting in the degeneracy of Sinhala society and its rapid descent to barbarism". Life was paralysed in Colombo and southern parts of the Island. Tamil neighbourhoods and houses were in ruins. Patricia Hyndman of the LAWASIA has pointed out:

> Members of the police and armed forces had stood by and allowed attacks to be made on the Tamil people. Even worse, in some cases they had actively participated in the attacks. There had been a pattern to the violence...gangs were transported from

> outside the districts. They had electoral lists with them from which Tamil houses, shops and addresses were identified.

The ethnic polarisation, which was gradually building up, increased in intensity after July 1983. Even progressive Tamils belonging to radical trade unions and leftist parties were made conscious that "regardless of their political ideology, they were identified as Tamils and not as Sri Lankans". Jean Arasanayagam, the well-known Burgher writer, married to a Sri Lankan Tamil, and who spent few days in a refugee camp in Kandy, mentions the effect of the ethnic conflict on the two major communities as follows:

> To me the postscript of the refugee camp is this: You stretch your hand in greeting, in friendship, and the person before you refuses to take it. It is as if the arm hangs loose, jointless, fallen out of a sling.. You keep stretching your hand out into space and you feel that there are a million hands that are not going to hold your hand anymore.

The prolonged conflict since 1983 (with occasional cease-fires in between) resulted in internal displacement as well as flow of refugees to India and to other parts of the world. We have divided the affected people into three categories: 1. Internally displaced people within Sri Lanka; 2. Sri Lankan Refugees and nationals in Tamil Nadu and 3. Sri Lankan Tamils living abroad. Refugees in Tamil Nadu will be discussed in detail in subsequent chapters.

Internally Displaced

Internal displacement in Sri Lanka was the consequence of ethnic cleansing. It resulted in a devastating transformation. As a Brookings study pointed out:

> Families lost their homes and livelihoods, leaving behind all they had cherished... Too often children lost their access to education and forced to child labour, sexual exploitation or recruitment into armed groups. Internal displacement shatters lives.

In Sri Lanka, the border controlled by the Government and the Tigers frequently changed as a result of fluctuating fortunes of war. The civilians living in these areas were subjected to cycles of violence, they were caught in the crossfire; they were rendered homeless and were displaced several times. Two illustrations are given below to substantiate this point. When the Sri Lankan army started moving towards Jaffna in the second half of 1995, the Tigers forced the people of Jaffna to move to Vadamarachi, Thenmaradchi and Vanni areas, where 300,000 people were displaced. They were forced to live in miserable conditions. As the University Teachers of Human Rights (UTHR) put it: "By 16 November, the city of Jaffna for the first time in 600 years, was completely empty. The trauma was extremely painful, both mentally and physically". Regarding the Tigers' role in the exodus from Jaffna, the UTHR report stated:

> The roots of the exodus must be sought in the character of the LTTE's politics, its unchanging agenda of totalitarian power, its absence of concern for the people, and its duplicity resulting from a historical inability to negotiate as part of a political process.

The second example of the lack of concern for the civilian population was the warning given to the people by the Tigers on November 10,1989 to evacuate Vavuniya. It is estimated that nearly 1,00,000 people joined the exodus. Panic gripped the town, people vacated their homes in a hurry, and traders pulled down their shutters, government offices closed and banks dealt with long queues of people desperately in need of money. Five days later, the LTTE thanked the people for their spontaneous response and asked them to return to Vavuniya.

The internally displaced people are those persons, who, as a result of persecution, armed conflict and violence, have been forced to abandon their homes and leave their usual place of residence, but remain within the country. Exact details of the ethnic breakdown of the internally displaced people are not available, but at the beginning of the Fourth Eelam War, it was estimated that 78 per cent of them were Tamils, 13 per cent Muslims and 8 per cent Sinhalese. What was deplorable was the fact that the Welfare Centers housed nearly 75,000 children who were under five years. And, as stated earlier, caught between the inhuman army and the ruthless LTTE, the hapless people had become pawns in the military games played by the warring parties. From the human rights angle, the displaced persons were the most vulnerable. As the *World Report, 1999* of the Human Rights Watch had pointed out:

> The link between forced displacement and Human rights is a crucial one. human rights violations are a principal root cause of forcible displacement. The human rights of the displaced refugees and internally displaced persons alike are frequently violated and threatened while they are displaced, and respect for fundamental human rights is a key factor in the search for a durable solution to any situation of displacement.

The Vanni area, which was the bone of contention between the Army and the Tigers, was one of the worst affected in Sri Lanka. A Christian delegation, which visited this region, a few years ago, pointed out that out of the population of 4,90,000, the displaced number was 3,05,000 and children under 18 years were estimated to be around 1,62,000. Some people were living under trees. Sanitary conditions were awful. Proper drinking water had become a luxury. A Report of the US Committee on Refugees had described the conditions of the people in Vanni area as follows: "The tens of thousands of displaced persons are at a high risk as the Government will not provide them with food aid, allegedly because it views them as sympathetic to the LTTE".

The agony and suffering of the internally displaced people is graphically described by Rohini Hensman. She narrates the poignant story of Anna's family. Anna's father pointed out the irony that "for two years, between 1983 and 1985, they were living in the very same camps, when their home in Dehiwela was attacked and all their belongings burned". The family moved to Batticaloa and slowly rebuilt its lives. They are back now in the camps, having lost everything for the second time, reduced to destitution once again". Anna's mother remarked:

> The problem is that neither the armed forces nor the Tigers are the least bit concerned about people...They are fighting for their own reasons... In Colombo, they wanted to kill us, because we were Tamil; in Batticaloa they wanted to kill us because I speak Sinhala and they thought that I was Sinhalese. There is no freedom anywhere in this country. What we need is peace, not Eelam.

During my visit to Colombo in December 1999, the UNHCR officials narrated the gist of a conversation between refugee women and representatives of OXFAM. One refugee woman remarked:

> Our problem is not a shortage of cooking pots or shelter. Our problem is the war. If you offer cooking pots, we will take them. But if you ask what you can really do for us we will say, help stop the fighting. If you can do anything to bring peace, we will be able to take care of ourselves and stop being a burden to you.

The UNHCR was doing commendable work among the IDPs during this period. Its presence dates back to 1987, when the India-Sri Lanka Accord was signed and its activities were linked to repatriation of refugees from India. With the beginning of the Second Eelam War in 1990, the UNHCR was requested by Colombo to work among the Internally Displaced Persons. The UNHCR operations "help mitigate the negative consequences of displacement and facilitate the return and re-settlement of displaced persons". It functioned in six districts – Kilinochi, Mullaithivu, Mannar, Vavuniya, Trincomalee and Jaffna – both in the "cleared areas" under the control of the Government and in the "uncleared areas", where the LTTE was dominant. The UNHCR worked in close collaboration with the Government and the UN agencies like the UNDP, UNICEF and ICRC.

Human Rights Violations

The negative side of the Fourth Eelam War needs to be highlighted. The Amnesty International, Human Rights Watch and the International Crisis Group have published detailed accounts of the human rights violations during those horrendous days. The UN estimates of civilian deaths in the final months of fighting range between 40,000 and 70,000, with an estimated 1,50,000 killed over almost 30 years of war, marked by brutal atrocities on both sides. High-ranking Government officials, including the Sri Lankan President and the Chief of the Army Staff, have refuted and dismissed these allegations as false. However, it is crystal clear that the war against the Tigers degenerated into a war against Tamil civilians. Schools, hospitals, orphanages, temples and churches were subjected to aerial bombings. Heavy artillery and rocket launchers were used to bring about devastation. Dr. Daya Somasundaram, Professor in Jaffna Medical College, has described the "collective trauma" suffered by the people in Vanni as follows:

> A population of 3,00,000 underwent multiple displacements, deprivation of water, food, medical care and basic needs, caught between the shellings and bombings of the State forces and the LTTE, which forcibly recruited men, women and children to fight on the front lines and held the rest hostage.

The University Teachers of Human Rights (UTHR), in a special report titled "Let them speak: Truth about the Sri Lanka's Victims of War" has blamed both the Army and the Tigers for the collective trauma. To quote:

> Both sides treated truth as an enemy. Outsiders who could bear witness to the events were kept out and silenced; dissent on either side was crushed; the

> poor and the powerless were treated as cannon fodder and in the case of Tamil civilians, ultimately locked up to prevent them from revealing what they had experienced. As the Report notes, Sri Lanka's war against truth has grave implications for the future of democracy.

Unfortunately, the Government of Sri Lanka got embroiled in a war of words with UN organizations about the alleged violations of human rights. Unhappy with the policies and programmes of the government, the European Union decided to discontinue tariff concessions to the garment and apparel industry, known as Generalised System of Preferences (GSP), to the tune of US Dollars 150 million per year. The Obama Administration in the United States also announced that it would review the trade tariff concessions linked to the workers' rights. More significantly, the stand-off between the United Nations and the Sri Lankan Government led to increasing international isolation of Sri Lanka. When the Secretary General of the United Nations met representatives of the Sri Lankan Government in 2009, the Sri Lankan Government committed itself to ensure the political and economic empowerment of the people of northern Sri Lanka. Mahinda Rajapaksa expressed his firm determination to go ahead with the implementation of the 13th Amendment as well as to begin a fresh dialogue with political parties, including Tamil parties. What is more, the President reiterated his strong commitment to the promotion and protection of human rights, in keeping with international human rights standards and Sri Lanka's international commitments. The UN Secretary General, on his part, underlined the importance of accountability process for addressing violations of international humanitarian and human rights law. The Government assured that it would take measures to address these grievances.

Despite these promises, no steps were taken by the Sri Lankan Government to investigate human rights violations and war violations. It was in this backdrop that the UN Secretary General decided to constitute an experts panel to report within four months what steps should be taken to ensure that Sri Lanka fulfills its commitments. The decision to constitute an Eminent Persons Group to advise him on human rights situation in Sri Lanka was greeted with vehement protests, including a demonstration and siege before the UN offices in Colombo and a fast unto death by a member of the cabinet. Sri Lankan Foreign Minister, G.L. Peiries, went to the extent of saying that the members of the panel will not be issued visas to visit Sri Lanka. In order to blunt mounting international criticism, the Sri Lankan Government appointed a three-member "Lessons Learnt and Reconciliation Commission". According to knowledgeable critics, the Commission did not have the mandate, means or independence to conduct proper investigation. It is also necessary to mention that the Sri Lankan Government constituted an independent international group of eminent persons to assist the Human Rights Commission. The members of that group included well-known Indian jurist, Justice Bhagwati. A few weeks later, the eminent persons group withdrew from its observer role because of flaws in the working of the Commission. Among other human rights violations that took place during this period, mention should be made of the assassination of Lasantha Wickrematunge, the editor of the *Sunday Leader,* the detention under the Prevention of Terrorism Act of Tissainayagam, former editor of the *Northeastern Herald* for his fearless reporting of the government's anti-democratic policies, and the attack on private TV channels like *Siyatha* for supporting opposition groups. The issues relating to war crimes and accountability continue to be ignored, though there had been change of governments in Sri Lanka.

The well-known Sri Lankan human rights activist, Jeevan Thyagarajah, has highlighted that there are certain basic standards of human rights protection. These are: 1. Nurturing of unity in cultural, religious and ethnic diversity, 2. Realising social justice by enshrining the rights of the vulnerable and marginalised groups, and 3. Ensuring democratic participation and the rule of law. Jeevan Thyagarajah has written that the Government's duty is not to "defend its human rights record, but to defend human rights". Highlighting the need for ethnic reconciliation, Jeevan Thyagarajah poignantly writes: "Wars are crimes. No war is just if you have to kill, maim, displace and terrorise. Our history since 1971 has narratives of our failure to prevent dissent from becoming violent. We need to remind ourselves of several Presidential Commissions awaiting implementation of recommended steps including prosecution due to disappearances. Human rights cannot be selective in its memory".

While solemnly affirming to protect and promote human rights, in actual practice Sri Lanka had been backsliding. A long promised Right to Information Bill was enacted in June 2016. The Parliament constituted an office under the Missing Persons Act, to assist families of the disappeared in searching missing relatives, but its record is abysmal. The Prevention of Terrorism Act has not yet been repealed; it is still used to arrest and detain suspects. Torture and other ill-treatment in police stations still continue. Violence against ethnic and religious minorities and human rights defenders has become the order of the day. What is more, the politics of Sri Lanka is once again getting embroiled into competitive one-upmanship to uphold the rights and aspirations of the majority Sinhalese community.

Most Vulnerable

Among the most vulnerable are the overseas migrant workers, mostly female and nearly 70,000 war widows in the north and the east. It has been estimated that there are nearly one million Sri Lankans employed overseas, especially in the Middle East. Many remained at "risk of abuse at every stage of the migration cycle, from recruitment and transit, to employment, repatriation and reintegration. More than a third of Sri Lankan migrants are domestic workers, almost exclusively female".

According to the country summary on Sri Lanka published by Human Rights Watch in January 2017, "many continued to face long working hours, with little rest, delayed and unpaid wages, confinement in the work place, and verbal, physical and sexual abuse."

Mention should also be made about the pathetic and deplorable conditions of nearly 70,000 war widows in the Tamil areas of Sri Lanka. One consequence of the ceasefire agreement between the Government and the Tigers in 2002 was Prabhakaran's decision to permit guerrillas to get married and start family life. Many got married and made a new beginning in their lives. But when the war resumed in 2006, Prabhakaran recalled them and in the subsequent war, most of them were killed, leaving behind nearly 70,000 widows with one or two children.

I had repeatedly requested the Tamil Nadu unit of the BJP to send a fact-finding team to Sri Lanka to address their problems and start programmes of self-employment. My appeal had fallen on deaf ears and these women, in the prime of their lives, continue to remain an orphaned community. There are cases of few women taking to prostitution to earn a living. Equally distressing is the fact that some of them are getting converted to Islam and have become second or third wives of Muslim husbands. In a conversation with me, Ram Kumar, associated with the Sri Lankan Tamil newspaper, *Veerakesari,* mentioned that the newspaper carries several advertisements relating to change of names, for example Padma to Fathima, obviously after conversion to Islam. Equally relevant, Ram Kumar pointed out that it is easier for Muslim women to get jobs as housemaids in Middle Eastern countries. The *Visva Hindu Parishad should* immediately constitute an Enquiry Committee to report on the situation and take remedial steps.

The International Crisis Group, in a report published in July, 2017, summed up the problems faced by these unfortunate women. They include

> rape and sexual violence, the deaths of family members, forced recruitment and killings by the Liberation Tigers of Tamil Eelam (LTTE) and destruction of homes and communities. The legacy of war continues to impose hardships, particularly on conflict-affected women. Lack of information on missing relatives, displacement from their land, economic deprivation, psychological trauma, vulnerability to sexual violence and exploitation plus a militarized environment that reinforces much of the above.

Equally unfortunate is the fact that women's issues do not receive the attention of political parties. Even the Tamil National Alliance (TNA), which proclaims that it supports truth and accountability has "generally given little attention to these issues, despite having the most MPs from conflict-affected *areas*" So deep is the patriarchal attitude of the Tamil leaders.

Sri Lankan Tamil Diaspora

Sri Lankans – Tamils, Sinhalese, Muslims and Burghers – had always been migratory. *According to the Encyclopedia of Sri Lankan Diaspora* published by the National University of Singapore, the Sri Lankan Diaspora is estimated to be approximately three million. They moved out of their motherland during the colonial and post-colonial periods. Their contribution to the host societies in the fields of economic and intellectual life is out of proportion to their number. It must, however, be highlighted that the post-independence years witnessed large scale migration and this was triggered by the worsening of ethnic relations in Sri Lanka. An important consequence was the burgeoning of the number of Sri Lankan Tamils who had to leave the country. In 2011, it was estimated that one out of eight Sri Lankans lived outside Sri Lanka. The main concentration of Sri Lankan diasporic communities are found in India, Malaysia, Singapore, Brunei, Darussalam in South and Southeast Asia; in the Gulf states in West Asia; in the United Kingdom, the Netherlands, France, Germany, Switzerland, Italy, Norway Sweden, Denmark, Portugal, Russia and East European countries in Europe; and in Australia and New Zealand in Australasia.

It is necessary to highlight the inter-relationship between the Diaspora and their motherland. Does the Sri

Lankan Tamil Diaspora, scattered in different parts of the world, reflect the feelings and aspirations of their kinfolk in Sri Lanka.? In what ways and to what extent can the Sri Lankan Tamil Diaspora influence the political and economic developments in their homeland?

In his absorbing novel, *Reef,* Romesh Gunesekhere, Sri Lankan Anglian writer, narrates the dilemma of living in a "splendid paradise". Triton, the character through whom Gunesekhere tells the gripping story, finally migrates to London and becomes the owner of a restaurant. The novel begins with Triton's encounter with a Tamil refugee boy, whom he meets in the latter's first night of employment in a petrol station. The boy knows only Tamil and requests Triton to speak to his boss over telephone. "Boss won't understand. You speak, please you know, please". The boy was born in Silavattuturai, once a "divers' paradise", but now "a landmark for gun-runners in a battle zone of army camps and Tigers". The Tamil boy wants to know whether he too "could become a restaurant owner in London. He was painting a dream. Will his dream ever be fulfilled? Or will he also become an unwelcome alien, moving from country to country in search of a secure job and a life of dignity?"

Victims of Human Trafficking

The UNHCR Report, *The State of the World's Refugees, 1995* describes in detail the ramifications of trafficking of Sri Lankan Tamil refugees. The educated Jaffna Tamil had always been migratory. Jaffna exported manpower for white collar jobs and professions even during the colonial period. As a consequence, Jaffna was known as the "post office economy". During the early 1980s, the majority of Sri Lankan Tamils seeking asylum in Europe and the Americas consisted of highly qualified professionals from middle classes; they could easily migrate to the West, with the assistance of friends and relatives settled abroad. As the ethnic conflict escalated, more and more people from all strata of society wanted to migrate to Western countries. In 1988, according to UNHCR, 8,000 Sri Lankans applied for asylum in Europe. By 1991, the figure had gone up to 24,000. The expenditure involved also shot up. In 1985, the process of travelling to Europe from Sri Lanka cost approximately US $ 1,000. By 1985, the figure had gone up to US $ 10,000. In order to leave Jaffna, when it was under the control of the Tigers, "exit tax" had to be paid to the LTTE. Clever and unscrupulous travel agents in Colombo further fleeced the gullible Tamils. The travel agents made flight reservations "on circuitous routes from Sri Lanka to other countries, informing the customers how to get on board a flight without necessary documentation, and how best to avoid deportation once they had arrived at their intended destination". The UNHCR Report adds:

> With the tightening of immigration and asylum controls in the richer states, the agents have also been able to diversify their business activities, providing would-be refugees with false documents and ready-made atrocity stories intended to prove that the asylum seeker had a genuine fear of persecution at home. In addition, the Sri Lankan agents have developed links with traffickers in Europe (commonly known as "schleppers" or people smugglers), whose function is to get would-be refugees from the countries of Western and Central Europe, where entry regulations are relatively lax, into the States of Western

> Europe, where the arrival of foreign nationals is more strictly controlled. The techniques which such smugglers used to deliver their human cargo are extremely dangerous. On a number of occasions, Sri Lankan Tamils have been found drifting on life rafts in Baltic Sea, near the Danish coast, apparently dropped off by Polish, Estonian and Latvian fishing vessels.

Prof. Valentine Daniel's report corroborates the UNHCR account. I have quoted Valentine Daniel extensively because the narratives portray the tragedy that has befallen the Sri Lankan Tamil community. According to Daniel:

> There are cases known to the London-based Joint Council for the Welfare of Immigrants in which middle men – also Tamils - have abandoned groups at transit points in such faraway places as Bangkok and Nairobi, after these same middlemen absconded with the 5000 pounds of "set up money" they received from their charges. Such a middleman takes them to an apartment or a room, tells them to stay put – lest they be caught by authorities until he makes arrangements for the next leg of the journey en route to London or some other Western capital. The room of the apartment in question is locked from outside to ensure double protection. The anxious and the frightened group waits, at times for days, until hunger and/or suspicion gets the better of them, and

> they break loose or start screaming for help. Some such desperate and penniless escapees are then offered by yet another set of racketeers, the opportunity of becoming drug carriers as means of buying their way back on the road to asylum.

In June 1998, I met Selvi, who was born in Jaffna and had come to Toronto after overcoming many obstacles. She was the only child of her parents. Her father died in 1988 during IPKF operations. Her mother died a year later. By 1989, Jaffna had come under LTTE control. She paid three sovereigns to the LTTE as "exit tax" and reached Colombo. After working for a few years as a domestic servant, Selvi decided to migrate to Canada. She contacted a travel agent, who gave her a false passport and a false visa on payment of Sri Lankan rupees equivalent to Canadian Dollars 25,000. On her first venture, Selvi and five others were detained in Dhaka by the immigration authorities and sent back to Colombo. Six months later, she went to Singapore and reached Toronto via New York. When I met her in the Siva temple, a familiar haunt of the Sri Lankan Tamil Hindus on weekends, she was awaiting a final decision on her application for asylum in Canada.

From 1983 to 1987, Tamil asylum seekers constituted about 8.5 per cent of all persons seeking asylum in Europe. The largest number went to West Germany, followed by France, Switzerland, United Kingdom, Netherlands, Denmark, Sweden and Italy. By December 1987, approximately 70,000 Tamils had sought asylum in Europe.

Tamils were the largest group of asylum seekers in Europe after Iranians. Though their number was small, in smaller countries, the Tamils were a visible group. Many Tamils used the infamous "Berlin gap" and underground rail link between East and West Berlin. The number of asylum seekers peaked in 1989 - 1991, when 43,000 persons applied for asylum.

Soon after the horrible incidents in July 1983, most of the European countries considered Tamils as a persecuted group, deserving sympathy and assistance. However, over the years, official attitudes have changed. Sri Lankan Tamils have become one of the most controversial communities in Europe. They have been made to feel that they are an unwanted lot. Right-wing politics has been in the upswing and the vested interests perceive the Tamils as a threat to their livelihood. In Germany, foreigners in general, and refugees in particular, became targets of "neo-Nazi and proto-fascist skinheads". In 1992, there were about 1800 anti-*auslander* (anti-foreigner) attacks, 16 of which were fatal – a "reflection of the growth of the right-wing extremists or neo-Nazis". Germany has started deporting illegal Sri Lankan Tamil immigrants back to Sri Lanka. The first batch of 20 Sri Lankan Tamils arrived in Colombo in March 2000. Some of them had stayed in Germany for more than nine years. Norway also wanted to repatriate Sri Lankan nationals who had not obtained the right of residence. An agreement to this effect was signed with Sri Lanka in early April 2000.

Canada has, relatively, the most liberal provisions of immigration and asylum. Naturally, it became the preferred destination for Sri Lankan Tamils. What is more, in Canada, asylum is the first step towards citizenship and eventual integration. The Canadian Government was sympathetic and adopted special measures to assist the Tamils. A Sri Lanka programme was started which allowed persons affected by the events of July 1983 to get asylum in Canada. Unlike Canada,the United States is very strict. The miniscule number of Tamils receiving asylum in the United States is the consequence of an unsympathetic and over vigilant Government in Washington.

The Sri Lankan Tamil communities abroad are highly politicised. They not only internationalised the ethnic conflict, they also financed the Tiger war machine. Discriminated against by successive Sinhalese dominated governments, the Tamils, who left Sri Lanka, were the torch bearers of Tamil nationalism. They also believed that the Government and people of Tamil Nadu would provide solid backing to them. But what the Diaspora did not realise was the fact that despite the sympathy for the Sri Lankan Tamil cause, what finally determined the stance of the Dravidian parties in Tamil Nadu was the equation between the Centre and the State Government. It must be pointed that, during the worst days of the Fourth Eelam War, the DMK, which was in power in Tamil Nadu under the leadership of Karunanidhi went along with the policies and programmes of the Central Government for reasons of political expediency. The ultimate losers were the Sri Lankan Tamils.

During the early 1980s all militant groups had their following among the Diaspora. But gradually the non-LTTE groups got sidelined and the Tigers came to have a virtual monopoly. The Sri Lankan Tamils abroad were the major financiers of the LTTE and they bankrolled the Tiger cause. It is estimated that the Tamils in Switzerland contributed approximately seven million francs every year. From Canada, the LTTE got about eight million Canadian Dollars annually. Conscious of the vital role of the Sri Lankan Tamils abroad, Prabhakaran deputed some of his ablest colleagues like Kittu, Lawrence Thilagar and Suresh Manickavasagam to co-ordinate various activities like mobilizing the Tamil communities, fund-raising and propaganda. In addition, the Tamil intellectuals living abroad, like Visvanathan Rudrakumaran and Dr. Sornarajah, provided intellectual inputs for drafting LTTE position during the ceasefire negotiations.

The tide began to turn against the Tigers when the Government of India, following the assassination of Rajiv Gandhi, and many Western Governments began to look upon LTTE as a terrorist organisation. The Tigers suffered a serious setback when the US Government included the LTTE as one of the terrorist organizations and banned its activities. Attempts made by the Tigers to buy surface-to-air missiles and anti-aircraft guns from the United States were aborted by intelligence agencies. In Canada, the police began to crack down on their anti-social activities. According to DBS Jeyaraj, a few Tamils were engaged in a bitter struggle in Toronto to control the lucrative business in narcotics, extortion, smuggling, robbery etc. The *Toronto Star* carried a news item linking Tamil refugees with the forging of Canadian passports for a heroin smuggling ring. Suresh Manickavasagam, the co-ordinator of the World Tamil Movement, a front organization of the LTTE, was detained. In a path-breaking judgement, the Canadian Court rejected the appeal made by Suresh Manickavasagam against the deportation order under the provisions of the National Security Act. Justice Robertson held that Canada's right to protect itself from known and suspected terrorists outweighed the rights of the individual suspects.

With the decimation of the Tigers, the overseas Sri Lankan Tamils are in disarray. Non-LTTE militant groups, which were silenced during the war years, have started voicing their views in the open. After considerable soul-searching, those who realised that the armed struggle had only brought suffering and devastation to the Tamils, have formed an organisation called the Global Tamil Forum (GTF). Led by the highly respected Fr S J Emmanuel, Suren Surendran from Australia and Velupillai Kuhanendran from London, the GTF wants to explore the possibility of finding a peaceful solution to the ethnic problem within a united Sri Lanka. It has good equation with the Tamil National Alliance (TNA) and assisted the latter in the September 2013 elections to the Northern Provincial Council. Unfortunately, the popularly elected Chief Minister had absolutely no role in the rehabilitation of the IDPs or in the formulation and implementation of centrally sponsored developmental programmes. The GTF held regular discussions with the Sri Lankan leaders. The GTF is also trying to use the talents and resources of the Tamils Overseas and contribute its share to the economic development of the north and the east. However, its attempts to fix responsibility for the war crimes, punish the guilty and trace the missing persons have not so far borne much fruit. What is more distressing for the GTF is the fact that there is absolutely no progress in the critical area of devolution of power to the Tamil provinces.

Mention should also be made of the Trans-National Government of Tamil Eelam (TGTE) under the leadership of V Rudrakumaran. The TGTE still subscribes to an independent state of Tamil Eelam and is popular among sections of Tamil population, who still hold the view that the only solution to the ethnic conflict is parting of the ways and establishment of an independent State of Tamil Eelam. There are also minor organisations, one of which controls the website, Tamilnet and according to informed sources, lot of money which was at the disposal of the LTTE during its heydays. It needs to be highlighted that there is close nexus between the developments in Sri Lanka and the policies and programmes of the Tamils overseas. And as mentioned earlier, there is no light at the end of the tunnel. Difficult days are ahead both for Sri lanka and the Sri Lankan Tamil Diaspora. ❑

5 Sri Lankan Refugees in Tamil Nadu

> I want to go home, but home is the mouth of a shark, home is the barrel of the gun and no one would leave home unless home chased you to the shore unless home tells you to leave what you could not behind even it was human.
>
> No one leaves home until home is a damp voice in your ear saying leave, run now, I don't know what I have become.

—Maggie Wagner,
"Home", A Refugee Poem

The word refugee, as Sadako Ogata, former UN High Commissioner for Refugees, said

> tends to evoke images of sprawling camps housing large number of distressed and impoverished people, who had to escape from their own country at short notice and with nothing but the clothes on their back.

This statement reflected the reality of the majority of Sri Lankan Tamil refugees when they sought asylum in

Tamil Nadu after the communal holocaust in July 1983. Geographical contiguity, easy availability of boats and ethnic affinities made Tamil Nadu a natural choice when large sections of Sri Lankan Tamils were forced to leave their country. New Delhi and Chennai alike recognized the need to provide asylum and admitted them with sympathy and understanding. Unlike many European countries, there were no time-consuming bureaucratic procedures, nor were there any restrictions on the movement of the Tamil people. At the same time, as Prof. Nirmala Chandrahasan points out, there is a certain amount of ambiguity about their legal status. India has no formal refugee determination process.

Waves of Refugees

The Sri Lankan Tamils came to Tamil Nadu in four waves. The first exodus of refugees began on 24 July 1983 and continued till 29 July 1987. During this period, 1,34,053 Sri Lankan Tamils arrived in India. Following the India-Sri Lanka Accord, 1987, refugees began to return to Sri Lanka. Between 24 December 1987 and 31 August 1989, 25,585 refugees and non-camp Sri Lankan nationals returned to Sri Lanka by chartered ships. The remaining Tamils either returned to Sri Lanka without Government assistance or continued to stay in Tamil Nadu either with their relatives or by their own means. According to Sri Lanka watchers, the period witnessed large-scale movement of Sri Lankan Tamils to different parts of Europe and Canada. Except two camps, one in Mandapam and the other in Kottapattu in Trichy, all other camps were closed down.

The Second Eelam War between Colombo and the Tigers commenced in June 1990 and resulted in the second wave of refugees. After 25 August 1990, 1,22,000 Sri Lankan Tamil refugees came to Tamil Nadu. Of these, 1,15,600 were destitutes and were accommodated in refugee camps. The repatriation of refugees commenced on 20 January 1992. According to the UNHCR, 54,188 refugees were voluntarily repatriated to Sri Lanka by chartered ships and flights from 20 January 1992 to 20 March 1995.

The Third Eelam War commenced in April 1995 and once again, the refugees started pouring into Tamil Nadu. By 12 April 2002, 22,356 refugees had come in. They comprised 7,715 families, consisting of 9,720 adult males and 2,110 adult females, 2,283 male children, and 2,236 female children. The fourth wave of refugees to Tamil Nadu will be described later in the chapter.

The flow of refugees was a consequence of the Sri Lankan Army's operations in the LTTE-controlled areas. Most refugees took the Talaimannar - Rameshwaram route, while a few others came via Nacheguda - Rameshwaram route. The refugees trekked long distances, assembled in Talaimannar, paid huge amounts to boat operators and reached Rameshwaram. The sufferings of the Tamil refugees became evident when a boat capsized in the Palk Strait and 165 Sri Lankan Tamils were drowned in February 1997. This was the second such incident; in October 1996, another tragedy took place near Mannar Island, in which 14 lives were lost.

By end 2001, the flow of refugees had become a trickle. In September, 2001 it was 26, in October, 78; in November, 11 and in December, 6. It should be pointed out that most Sri Lankan Tamils who wanted to leave the island and who had the financial means had left for greener pastures in Europe, United States and Canada. Equally important, the Sri Lankan Navy began patrolling the Palk Strait and made it difficult for the boat operators to come to India. What is more, the Indian Navy and the Coast Guard also stepped up their vigil. According to informed sources, during this period, a few boat operators from Tamil Nadu began to smuggle scarce commodities to the Tigers like petrol and life-saving drugs and sometimes, in return journey they brought a few refugees. However, it was the Sri Lankan fishermen who ferried most of the refugees to Tamil Nadu. The Government of Tamil Nadu began to impound the boats which were used to transport the refugees. But it did not act as a deterrent. Every journey allowed the boat operators to make more money than the cost of the boat. In 1997-98, the transport fee became exorbitant and ranged from Rs.15000 to Rs. 30000 depending on the need of the refugees and the size of the boat. The boat operators also exploited the shallowness of the Palk Strait. They dropped the refugees in the sea very near the coast and asked them to wade through the water and report in the Mandapam camp.

Categories of Tamils from Sri Lanka

The Tamils who came from Sri Lanka can be divided into the following categories: 1. Refugees of Sri Lankan Tamil origin who live in the camps; 2. Refugees of Indian Tamil origin who live in the camps; 3. Refugees who live outside the camps; 4. Sri Lankan nationals; 5. Militant refugees in Special Camps and 6. Miscellaneous category.

Refugees in the Camps

As on July 1, 2016, according to the Policy Note, 2016-17, issued by the Tamil Nadu Government, as per data collected from the District Collectors, 19,388 families consisting of 63,649 persons, are staying in 107 refugee camps located in 24 districts in the State. The Policy Note does not make a distinction between Sri Lankan Tamil refugees and Indian Origin Tamil refugees and the figure includes both. The distinction between the two categories must be kept in mind. The Sri Lankan Tamils are as indigenous to the island as the Sinhalese are. And, what is more, they do not consider themselves to be part of the Indian Diaspora. They are part of Tamil Diaspora. The Tamils of Indian Origin are the descendants of those who went to Ceylon under the protective umbrella of the British Government to provide labour for the development of tea plantations and public works, like development of the Colombo port. According to informed sources, there are 29,500 refugees of Indian Tamil origin among the camp refugees. If you deduct the figure of the Indian Tamils, the number of Sri Lankan Tamil refugees works out to 34,149.

Refugees of Indian Tamil Origin

According to informed sources, there are 29,500 refugees of Indian Tamil origin in the camps. The legal distinction between the two groups has to be kept in mind, as large sections in this group would like to become Indian citizens. It should also be highlighted that a miniscule number among them has been conferred Indian citizenship under the Sirimavo-Shastri Pact of 1964, but they did not get repatriated to India before 1983. They came to India as refugees at a later date. There are also stateless people in this group i.e. those who are neither Indian citizens nor Sri Lankan citizens, and the third category is Sri Lankan citizens. The stateless among them can get Sri Lankan citizenship, if they go back to Sri Lanka.

Recognised Refugees outside the Camps

Some Si Lankan Tamils came by boat to Rameshwaram and informed the officials of the Rehabilitation Department that they did not want to stay in refugee camps as they could look after themselves economically. They were asked to register themselves in the police station, nearest to their place of residence and also get a refugee certificate from the District Collector's office. These refugees are not eligible for financial doles or other benefits provided by the Tamil Nadu Government. These people are recognised as non-camp refugees. According to the Policy Note of the Tamil Nadu Government, on the basis of data provided by the Q branch, there are 36,651 non-camp refugees in the State.

Sri Lankan Nationals

There were Sri Lankan nationals who came to India with valid travel documents. They stay in Tamil Nadu and live through their means. They are required to register themselves in the police station, but many do not do so. They use India as a transit point to migrate to other countries. They pose as Indian nationals, go to Nepal and proceed to Singapore, Bangkok and other Southeast Asian countries where, as Sri Lankan citizens, they get visa on arrival. Some of them have integrated with the local population in Tamil Nadu, have got Aadhar cards, registered themselves in the census and have acquired property. The Policy Note does not make a mention about these people, nor do we have reliable statistics about them.

Militants in Special Camps

Those Sri Lankans who are alleged to have militant links are kept in a Special Camp in Tiruchirapalli. According to the Policy Note, as on I July 2016, 14 Sri Lankan Tamils are lodged in the Special camp under Section 3 (2) (e) of the Foreigners Act, 1946. Their movements are restricted; they are provided with cooked food worth Rs. 100/- per day. The living conditions in these camps are abominable and the National Human Rights Commission has drawn the attention of the State Government to improve the living conditions.

R.K. Radhakrishnan, correspondent of the ***Frontline,*** has written that Special Camps are a "euphemism for open-air prisons".The media has also reported that the inmates in these camps occasionally resort to hunger strikes to improve their conditions.

Miscellaneous Category

Some Sri Lankan Tamils who are citizens of European countries have come to live in Tamil Nadu. R. Sundaralingam, former Chief Superintendent of Police, Northern Province, Sri Lanka was deputed to Interpol in Paris, where he acquired French citizenship. He came to Chennai some years ago to give lectures on the narcotics trade. He and his wife have taken to religious and cultural life of Chennai as fish to water. Sundaralingam informed me that he regularly extends his visa in order to continue to live in Chennai. Nirmala Chandrahasan, former Professor of Law in Colombo University, belongs to another category. Daughter of Naganathan, well-known Federal Party leader and wife of Chandrahasan, founding father of OfERR (Organisation for Eelam Refugees Rehabilitation), Nirmala belongs to the well-known Hensman family, who migrated to India under British rule and became Indian citizens. Nirmala has acquired Overseas Indian Citizenship, while remaining a Sri Lankan citizen.

Flow of Refugees

The flow of refugees is closely linked to the violence unleashed in Sri Lanka against civilian population. The twists and turns in Sri Lanka's policy had their inevitable impact on Sri Lankan refugees. It should also be mentioned that the Sri Lankan Tamils are a highly politicized group and the refugees "were the warm waters in which militant fishes thrived". The competitive nature of Tamil Nadu politics, with the two Dravidian parties competing with one another in championing the Sri Lankan Tamil cause, and New Delhi's policy of arming Tamil militants paved the way for setting up of militant camps in different parts of Tamil Nadu. As time went on, for a variety of reasons, the LTTE emerged as a close-knit, disciplined and ruthless organization. The Tigers had twelve units in Tamil Nadu to fuel their war machine. These are: 1. Procurement of explosives – Dharmapuri; 2. Arms and ammunition manufacturing – Coimbatore; 3. Manufacturing of explosives – Salem; 4. Military uniforms-Erode; 5. Coastal area from where supplies were sent to Jaffna- Vedaranyam; 6. Transit area- Madurai; 7. Landing area for supplies from abroad – Nagapattinam; 8. Area where refugees arrived and militants recruited- Rameshwaram; 9. Communication centre – Thanjavur; 10. Trade in silver, gold and narcotics - Tuticorin; 11. Liaison with political parties – Chennai and 12. Treatment of wounded guerrillas – Trichy. What was tragicomic about the whole situation was the fact that New Delhi was trying to conceal the presence of militant camps in Tamil Nadu. As time went on, the militants became a law unto themselves and the peace and tranquility of Tamil Nadu was vitiated by gun-toting Tamil militants. As M.R. Narayana Swamy has described:

> All Tamil groups had their own camps, which were virtually prohibited zones for outsiders. One could do anything in these secluded fortresses, no question asked. Even when some one was tortured to death, the screams would reach nowhere. If the victim died, he would be simply buried there or in the barren vicinity.

The dastardly assassination of Rajiv Gandhi by the suicide squad of the LTTE swung the pendulum to the other extreme. Tamil Nadu - people and political parties alike – are yet to recover from the trauma. A Report of the Jesuit Refugee Service, which visited Tamil Nadu in March 1994, mirrored accurately the feelings of the people: "Many of the locals, including Church people, now view their Tamil brothers and sisters no longer as refugees, but as terrorists or militants". Presumably spurred by security considerations, the Government of Tamil Nadu over-reacted. Jayalalitha, then Chief Minister, demanded immediate action so that all Sri Lankan Tamils could be sent back. To quote, "I appeal, rather demand that the Centre should take immediate action so that all Sri Lankan Tamils are sent back – (it) should take place immediately". The Government restricted the facilities for higher education for the refugees and their movement from the camps was tightly monitored. The Government of Tamil Nadu began to exert pressure on New Delhi to get the refugees repatriated to Sri Lanka.

Controversy over Repatriation

The repatriation commenced in January 1992. There was an outburst of criticism that India was "pressurising" the refugees to leave; repatriation was "involuntary", and since peace had not yet returned to Sri Lanka, the repatriates would not be safe in the island. The NGOs working among the refugees in India and human rights organisations like ***Asia Watch,*** alleged that the hapless refugees were being "forced" to leave and that their signatures had been obtained in option forms (unfortunately the forms were printed in English), the contents of which they did not know. According to ***Asia Watch,*** the repatriates "faced direct and indirect coercion to return home, including arbitrary arrest, withdrawal of stipends and food rations". Further, no international agency was permitted to visit the refugee camps to monitor whether the system was "voluntary". The refugees had also no "reliable means" of ascertaining the actual conditions in their villages in Sri Lanka.

Prof. Asha Hans visited the refugee camps in Tamil Nadu during this period. She interviewed a large number of refugees. According to Asha Hans, "The excellent Indian record of providing refuge to numerous neighbours has been blemished by the push factors used in repatriating Sri Lankan refugees". The villain, according to Asha Hans, was the Government of Tamil Nadu. The option forms, circulated among the refugees, which was in English language, did not contain any provisions as to whether the refugees wished to return or not. The Government drew up unrealistic schedules, giving the refugees three to four days to leave for the transit camps. Ration cards were withdrawn and educational facilities curtailed. Security within and outside the camps were tightened, and many refugees could not go out to work. When the refugees complained, according to Asha Hans "some of them were beaten up in the process". As a security measure, the Government of Tamil Nadu embarked upon a thorough re-organisation of the camps, and the refugees were relocated in camps depending upon the area from which they came from Sri Lanka. These criticisms were valid, especially the accusation that the refugees were repatriated to Sri Lanka at a time when the security situation in the island was uncertain. In fact, when the Third Eelam War commenced in April 1995, many refugees who were repatriated to Sri Lanka came back to Tamil Nadu as refugees. In the course of my visit to the camps housing internally displaced persons in 2001 in Sri Lanka, I came across many refugee families who were stranded in these welfare centres. These repatriates from Tamil Nadu were unable to return home because their villages were located in the war zones. In other words, repatriation, for them, meant transfer from one refugee camp to another. By May 1992, 23,000 refugees were repatriated to Sri Lanka.

The UNHCR also criticised forced repatriation. The UNHCR representative, Hasheed Furkhan, who visited India, declared that repatriation did not take place according to an "internationally accepted procedure". Sadako Ogata, the Head of the UNHCR, took up the matter directly with the Government of India.

Following international concern about the repatriation process and continuing insecurity in Sri Lanka, repatriation of refugees was temporarily suspended. Muchkund Dubey, then Foreign Secretary, suggested to Prime Minister Narasimha Rao that the best way to come out of the dilemma was to request the UNHCR to monitor the voluntariness of repatriation. Negotiations soon started and, in July 1992, an Agreement was reached which allowed the UNHCR a token presence in Chennai with access to refugees at the point of departure, in the transit centres, but not in the camps. The decision to permit the UNHCR to operate from Chennai and monitor the repatriation process saved New Delhi from considerable embarrassment.

The international context was also congenial. The end of the Cold War witnessed the return of about 2.4 million refugees worldwide to their homes. To quote an UNHCR Report:

> The ideal environment for the return of the refugees is one in which the causes of the flight have been definitely and permanently removed – for example, the end of the Cold War or a change of Government which

> brings an end to violence and persecution. The ideal is rarely achieved, instead refugees return to places where political disputes will simmer and occasionally boil over, where fragile ceasefires break down, are repaired, and then break down again, when agreements are broken and trust is removed. The great majority of returnees in the early 1990s have been going back to a situation of this kind – for example, in Angola, in Mozambique, Cambodia, Sri Lanka and Afghanistan.

The UNHCR officials, as stated earlier, are not permitted to visit refugee camps; however, any refugee can contact the UNHCR if he/she wants to do so. According to UNHCR, they conducted interviews with 70 per cent of refugees to verify the voluntary nature of their return; they were convinced that the refugees were not subjected to any "overt coercion". Only 19 families, comprising 68 persons, complained that they were being repatriated "under duress". They were permitted to return to the camps, following UNHCR's initiative.

By May 1995, according to UNHCR statistics, 51,185 refugees returned to Sri Lanka. It was noted that, 52 per cent of these refugees had gone back for reasons of family reunion; 17 per cent for reasons of employment and some others for education. Some stated that bad conditions in the camps prompted them to go back to Sri Lanka.

The UNHCR presence in Tamil Nadu has facilitated better co-ordination between India and Sri Lanka. The UNHCR has been functioning in Sri Lanka since 1987, and co-ordination between the two units, coupled with the co-operation of the bureaucracy on both sides, contributed to the overall success of the repatriation process. The UNHCR has been assisting refugees separated from their families by arranging reunion. As and when the UNHCR receives any complaints/ suggestions, concerning the refugee camps, it immediately brings the matter to the attention of the State Government and attempts to speed up the administrative machinery. For example, there are several cases of overflowing septic tanks, repair of toilets and replacing electric wires, which the UNHCR brought to the notice of the concerned authorities and got the repair work done.

The presence of the UNHCR in Chennai, though with a limited mandate, has enhanced the credibility of New Delhi in international forums. The Madras High Court in the case of P Nedumaran and S Ramdoss V The Union of India and The State of Tamil Nadu stated:

> In so far as the consent of the refugees is concerned, when there is a world agency to ascertain whether the consent is voluntary or not, it is not for the Court to consider whether the consent is voluntary or not. Nothing has been suggested against the competence or impartiality of the UNHCR in ascertaining the willingness of the refugees to go back.

The refugees are understandably uncertain about their future in Sri Lanka. This was amply demonstrated when the first batch of refugees left by ***M.V. Akbar*** from Chennai to Trincomalee on 20 January 1992. The LTTE condemned the repatriation as an "inhuman act", and hours before the ship reached Trincomalee, an LTTE ambush killed 20 Sri Lankan soldiers at Kuchchavali. The LTTE also blasted part of the Air Force Base in China Bay in Trincomalee harbour, killing eight soldiers. According to senior Government officials, who accompanied the repatriates, the panic-stricken Tamils immediately demanded that they should be taken back to Chennai. They refused their food rations and declared that they would not disembark in Trincomalee. The officials did not want to abort the maiden voyage; they assured the repatriates that no one would be compelled to get down in Trincomalee, those who wanted to return to Chennai would be taken back. When the ship finally reached Trincomalee, the repatriates found their friends and relatives waiting to receive them. All of them disembarked without any protest.

Life in the Refugee Camps

When the Sri Lankan Tamil refugees poured into Tamil Nadu at the end of July 1983, the Government of India and the Government of Tamil Nadu rose to the occasion. India's earlier experience with tackling the problems of the refugees came in handy. Makeshift camps sprang up in different parts of Tamil Nadu. As ***Asia Watch*** highlighted, "Abandoned schools, poultry farms, cremation grounds, warehouses, even open-air toilets, have been used to house the refugees. Many refugees, living along the coast, are housed in emergency storm shelters".

An office was set up in Mandapam, where the refugees were registered. The camp which was used for quarantining the Indian workers who migrated to Sri Lanka in the 19th and 20th centuries was converted into the landing space of the refugees. Food, clothing and medical facilities were provided. After few days, the refugees were sent to different parts of Tamil Nadu. The shelters in the camps, 10' by 10', were covered with asbestos sheets, which made them a virtual furnace in summer months.

While analysing the living conditions in the refugee camps, one fact has to be highlighted, that the refugees came from a poor country to a poorer country. But what made Tamil Nadu an attractive destination was the fact that there was no fear of insecurity in the State. In the initial years, the Sri Lankan Tamils were afraid of the army, in subsequent years, they were also afraid of the Tigers, who would forcibly take away their children, both boys and girls, and compel them to join the guerrillas.

The refugees were provided with free housing, free medical care and free education. Rice priced at 57 paise per kilo and sugar and kerosene at subsidised rates from the public distribution system were also provided to the refugees. The cash dole amounted to Rs. 150 for one member, Rs. 270 for two members, Rs. 345 for three members, Rs. 382 for four members and Rs. 562 for five members every fortnight. What must be highlighted is the fact that the local poor people who lived in nearby areas were not entitled to such benefits. For example, the local people had to pay Rs. 3.50 per kilo of rice from the public distribution system. In a noble gesture, the refugees were also permitted to work outside the camps to supplement their income, a facility which was not extended to the Chakma refugees from Bangladesh. In some cases, the family income was supplemented by remittances from relatives abroad.

These facts are mentioned, not to deny the refugees their due, but to set the record straight in the context of misguided criticism levelled by certain human rights organisations. The US Committee on Refugees, in its 1991 Report, has noted that "India has accorded a welcome to the Tamil asylum seekers that are as generous as any refugee group in Asia". During the 1980s the annual expenditure on the refugees worked out to

Rs. 15.50 crores. The expenditure was initially incurred by the State Government, and subsequently reimbursed by the Government of India.

As time went on, changes were brought about in the camps due to the efforts of the Government of Tamil Nadu, the NGOs working among the refugees and through their own initiatives, which made living conditions a little better. Among the NGOs, mention should be made of OfERR (Organisation for Eelam Refugees Rehabilitation), Jesuit Refugee Service, and ADRA India. Asbestos sheets, which covered the houses, were replaced by terracotta tiles; and in a few others, wooden ceilings have been put under the asbestos sheets. The refugees have expanded the living space by constructing additional rooms in the front or in the rear. Kerosene stoves have been replaced by gas stoves. There are fans of various kinds – ceiling fan, table fan and pedestal fans. Every house has a television set. Every family has a mobile phone. Drinking water has been made available. A common structure, where children could study, has been constructed. And in some camps, temples have come up so that the devout can offer prayers. Many refugees own bicycles, motorbikes and scooters.

Taking into consideration the rising cost of living, the Tamil Nadu Government has increased the financial doles for the refugees; it also took a major decision in June 2011, to extend all welfare schemes being implemented for the benefit of the people of Tamil Nadu to the Sri Lankan Tamils residing in the camps. The enhanced financial dole to the head of the family is Rs. 1,000, to each additional member above 12 years Rs. 750, children below 12 years Rs. 400. Every month, 20 kg of rice is provided free of cost and other essential commodities such as sugar, maida, sooji, wheat,etc are supplied at subsidised rates through the ration shops.

The decision to permit the refugees to work is definitely a blessing in disguise. Every able-bodied person gets work, though, unfortunately, in few cases, they have to contend with wages below the minimum prescribed by the Government. The more enterprising among them have come together and take contract for the demolition of old houses and brick-building. Many work as painters, masons and as helpers in construction sites. Women generally remain at home. According to NGOs working among the refugees, every male member, who works outside the camp, is able to earn around Rs. 1000 per day. Among other welfare schemes, mention should be made of issue of driving licenses, sewing machines to destitute women to augment their income, a revolving fund of Rs. 10,000 for women self-help groups, a monthly pension of Rs. 1,000 to destitute persons like widows, old and differently abled people, deserted wives and unmarried women. To meet expenses relating to funeral of the dead, an outright grant of Rs. 5000 is given. The relief amount to death by accident has been enhanced to Rs. 25,000/. An amount of Rs. 50,000 and 4 grams of gold for ***Thirumangalyam*** are given to girls about to be married. The gold for ***Thirumangalyam*** has been enhanced now from 4 grams to 6 grams. Pregnant women are given assistance of Rs. 12,000. In case of families with one girl child, a sum of Rs. 50,000 is deposited which will be given to the family at the end of twenty years. All Sri Lankans living in the camps and outside are covered by the Chief Minister's Comprehensive Health Scheme.

According to the Policy Note, 2016-17, a sum of 108.70 crore was spent on the refugees in 2015-16.

Achievements in Education

The most praiseworthy aspect of the refugee life in Tamil Nadu is the accomplishment in the field of education.

In no other country in the world have the refugees excelled in education as they have in Tamil Nadu. The credit for this remarkable phenomenon has to go to the perseverance of the refugees, the yeoman work done by NGOs like OfERR (Organisation for Eelam Refugees Rehabilitation) and the Jesuit Refugee Service and to a caring and sympathetic State Government. Every boy and girl of school-going age attends schools. Some of them, for economic reasons, drop out at a later stage, but, the drop-out rate among the refugees is less than among the local population. Another interesting aspect of education should be highlighted. In Sri Lanka from mid-1950s, ***Swabhasa*** **–** Sinhalese and Tamil – was introduced as the medium of instruction from primary to University level. Having come to Tamil Nadu, the refugees realised that English language is the passport to the outside world, and, therefore, those who can afford the fees send their children to English medium schools. Since there are no proper facilities for study in the living quarters in almost all the camps, a study centre has been constructed where the children can study after school hours. The NGOs assist the students with teaching kits and coaching, in addition to financial aid. It must be mentioned that the Jesuit Refugee Service regularly hold workshops for the teachers during summer vacation to improve the quality of education.

Sri Lankan Tamil students, both in the camps and outside, studying in Government and Government aided schools, are provided free education upto 12th standard. Further, they are provided with notebooks, textbooks, uniforms, noon meals, bus passes and laptop computers, free of cost. During 2015-16, 29,351 students were enrolled in various educational institutions.

Sri Lankan Tamil students are admitted in Arts and Science colleges, Professional colleges, Polytechnics and

Universities based on merit through the single window counselling system. Further orders have been issued to admit five Sri Lankan Tamil students in each hostel run for the BC, MBC and Adi Dravidar and Tribal students to pursue their higher education. 67 students have availed of the facilities in 2015-16. The Government is providing scholarship to those pursuing higher education, per annum, as follows: BA – Rs. 1,200, B.Sc – Rs. 1,250; MA –Rs. 1,330; M.Sc - Rs. 1,650; Diploma - Rs. 850; BE/B.Tech – Rs. 2,750; M.B.B.S/B.D.S. – Rs. 4,700- B.VSc – Rs. 1,400; BL – Rs. 860 and B.Sc (agri) – Rs. 2,850. During 2015-16, 597 students have availed of these scholarships.

The Government has also issued orders that cash awards be given to students who have secured first three places in 10th and 12th standard, both for boys and girls, in the refugee camps.

Another notable achievement is that girls outnumber boys in various sectors of education. Another redeeming feature is that the Government of Tamil Nadu has allotted a specific number of seats to Sri Lankan Tamils in institutions of higher learning. One of the admirable achievements of OfERR (Organisation for Eelam Refugees Rehabilitation) is that it counsels, encourages, and motivates Sri Lankan refugee children to give highest priority to education.

Negative Aspects of Refugee Lives

Certain negative trends in refugee camps need mention. Boys and girls get married very early, unlike in Sri Lanka where they get married in late 20s. Living together in camps lead to infatuation and early marriage; sometimes these marriages end in disaster and divorce. Alcoholism is rampant among the young and this leads to friction between parents and children. According to media reports, a few youngsters have been caught for smuggling narcotics to Sri Lanka.

Fourth Eelam War – Security Considerations Outweigh Humanitarian Concerns

The Fourth Eelam War was a fight to the finish. In order to minimize the flow of refugees into Tamil Nadu, the Sri Lankan Navy began to consolidate its hold on the Sri Lankan side of the Palk Bay. From Mannar, they began to move south, controlled Madhu Church, which was a transit point for refugees, consolidated its position in the outer islands and strengthened its hold in Jaffna and surrounding regions. The Indian Coast Guard, in its turn, increased vigil on the Indian side of the Palk Bay. When the war against the Tigers degenerated into a war against Tamil civilians, followed by frequent displacements, the Sri Lankan Tamils, caught between an inhuman army and a ruthless LTTE, underwent enormous suffering. Compounding the situation was Sri Lankan Government's decision not to allow the movement of food and medicines to Tamil Areas. In April 2008, I met a refugee, who had come in a boat to India from Mullaithivu along with few others. Lack of drinking water led to dehydration and death of his friends. The bodies were dumped into the sea. In a voice full of agony and anguish, the refugee said that every Tamil caught between Sri Lankan Army and the Tigers would have loved to come to Tamil Nadu as refugees, but they were unable to do so. In the highest forum available to me in New Delhi, I pleaded that the Government of India must take the initiative, and, along with the US and member states of European Union, enforce a ceasefire in Sri Lanka so that the innocent could be moved to a safer place. The war against the Tigers then can be continued. Response from the powers that be in New Delhi was not encouraging; they did not mind the loss of innocent civilian lives, what was more important was the destruction of the LTTE war machine. As a result, during the worst phase of the ethnic conflict - January 12, 2006 to January 4, 2010 - only 24,527 refugees could come to Tamil Nadu. In the normal course, it would have been a mass exodus of refugees. New Delhi's callous and indifferent attitude contributed to one of the worst tragedies of our times. On that occasion, I said, quoting Lady Macbeth, that our hands are also tainted with blood, and all the perfumes of Arabia will not sweeten our dirty hands.

Experiences of Refugees

The Greek philosopher Euripides made a poignant statement in 431 BC: "There is no greater sorrow on earth, than the loss of one's native land". The implications of this statement became evident when I started studying the problems of the refugees in Tamil Nadu. The Government of Tamil Nadu does not permit academicians to visit the camps for academic research. However, over the years, I came into contact with several refugees – men, women and children – and the NGOs working among them. My interaction with them has enabled me to have a better appreciation of their ways of life. I started admiring their resilience against heavy odds. And, above all, I began to empathise with their fears and hopes.

For the bureaucrats around the world, refugees are only an embarrassing statistic. In the Secretariat, the refugee is only a file, to be pushed from clerk to the officer, not human beings given to joys and sorrows, longings and aspirations. I felt that it was my duty to focus on the human angle. As Pamela Devoe has written: The refugee communities are

> often still in crisis, in trauma, due to their experiences in their original homeland. Many spend years in refugee camps; where births, marriages and deaths take place

> within the confines of this unnatural setting. Trauma continues in the initial stages of settling into a host country and adjusting to its often markedly different cultures.

Most refugees experience a void in their lives. Rajan Philips, a Sri Lankan refugee, who has become a Canadian citizen, explains:

> They are victims of a painful rupture between their immediate past and their immigrant present. The gap between their natal memories and their uprooted existence, not to mention the leap for most of them from tropical sunshine into the freezing winter, is almost unbearably unbridgeable.

Sikha Bose, while narrating the travails of the Chakma refugees, highlights a universal phenomenon:

> Fences and border patrols will not succeed in preventing the march of the people away from a place of insecurity to a place of relative security. As demonstrated by the Chakmas, unless their security is guaranteed, people will come and go, back and forth across the borderline, violating every rule of international and internal laws.

The most vulnerable section among the refugees is old people and women. Valentine Daniel narrates the story of a former school teacher, who was an eyewitness to the army's atrocities on civilian population:

> A man in his forties, a witness to "an atrocity" committed by soldiers in the

> north of Sri Lanka was interviewed by Daniel in a refugee camp in South India. The man goes in and out of total silence, abstinence from food and a disinterest in his environment to the point of not even reacting to danger. His niece, who took care of him, reported the incident of a burning ember falling of the hearth and setting fire to a chopping block. The flames from the burning wood ignited a line of clothes hung up to dry in the kitchen. As for her uncle, she said, "There he was near the door, where we had left him. He hadn't moved. He was looking straight at the fire, but hadn't moved."

Women are the worst victims not only in times of ethnic conflict, but also in refugee camps. Many have become widows, some have lost their children in the Eelam Wars; and, in some cases, children have joined the Tigers against the wishes of the parents. Husbands are almost invariably alcoholics; wife-beating is quite common; but, despite these disabilities, women continue to be the stabilizing force in the family life. Their hopes focus on their offspring; but their memories still revolve around the past. What Patricia Omidien and Juliene Lipson say about Afghan women is true of Sri Lankan Tamil women:

> Women spend their time every day for family to return from work or school; they wait for news; wait for some one to take them visiting; they wait to pray, and sometimes they wait to die.

The trauma of the Indian Tamils in the refugee camps is corroborated by the following incident. Maria Selvam, an up-country Tamil, with his wife, three daughters and one son, migrated to Vavuniya after the 1977 communal riots. After 1983, the family moved to Tamil Nadu as refugees. They were living in the Minnur Camp in the North Arcot district. Susivani, daughter of Maria Selvam, was admitted in Vadacherry School. She was an extremely bright student and was immensely popular among her teachers and friends. She passed her plus 2 in 1995 with good marks and was naturally eager to study further. But, she could not afford higher studies. Maria Selvam tried to persuade Susivani to take up employment as a housemaid in West Asia. Susivani was initially reluctant, but finally veered round, when her father told her that she could save money, return to India and join a college for higher studies. Susivani got herself repatriated to Colombo and from there, went to one of the Gulf countries as a housemaid. Like many others in the profession, she was sexually abused. Unable to bear the shame and humiliation, she scaled the walls of her employer's house and rushed to the Indian Embassy with an SOS that she be flown back to India. The officials of the Indian Embassy expressed helplessness because she was a Sri Lankan citizen. She approached the Sri Lankan Embassy and, after considerable difficulties, was flown back to Colombo. From Colombo she went to Vavuniya; misfortune dogged her and finally Susivani committed suicide.

The entrapment of the refugees in the camps is graphically illustrated by Lynellyn Long. One morning, Lynellyn met her refugee friends Chanthamom and her husband Khamsai. The conversation veered round to dreams.

> "Last night, I dreamt" he (Khamsai) begins hesitantly. "What" we ask again. "I dreamt of a cock that shat in a cage". We both burst out laughing. Chanthamom laughs so hard that he can barely speak. "Really" she asks incredulously, "Yes" he replies. We laugh again, but suddenly I realise he is right. The cock, shut in a cage cannot escape its own excrement.

Debt of Gratitude

When Tsunami struck the coastal regions of Tamil Nadu in December 2004 and brought death, destruction and devastation, the Sri Lankan Tamil refugees rose to the occasion and extended timely assistance. They acted as volunteers, removed the debris, disposed of the dead bodies, and provided solace and succour to the affected people. Their selfless work could be compared to the spontaneous response of the RSS volunteers who worked tirelessly in different parts of the State. In Tamil language, there is a beautiful phrase- ***Senchottukadam*** – which means debt of gratitude.

❐

6
Need for National Refugee Law

> Law is not a mausoleum. It is not an antique to be taken down, dusted, admired and put back on the shelf. It is essentially a social process, the end product of which is justice and hence it must change with changing social values. Otherwise, there will be estrangement between law and justice and law will cease to have legitimacy.
>
> **—P.N. Bhagwati, Motilal Padampet V The State of Uttar Pradesh**

South Asian countries are signatories to major international humanitarian and human rights covenants. Three countries – India, Pakistan and Bangladesh – are members of the governing body of the UNHCR. What is more interesting, as mentioned earlier, important South Asian leaders - M.A. Jinnah, Pervez Musharraf, Z.A. Bhutto, Manmohan Singh, I.K. Gujral, L.K. Advani and Ram Jethmalani were at one time refugees. Despite all these plus points, none of the South Asian countries is a signatory to the 1951 UN Convention on Refugees nor has ratified the 1967 Protocol. South Asian countries have also not enacted any separate national refugee law. As a result, the problems relating to the refugees are dealt with in an ***ad hoc*** basis.

There is one silver lining on the horizon. The UNHCR in India has taken the initiative to sensitise the intelligentsia about the problems of refugees in South Asian countries. Number of seminars and workshops have been organised in collaboration with Universities and organisations like (SAARCLAW) South Asian Association for Regional Cooperation in Law and Indian Centre for Humanitarian Law and Research (ICHLR). Informal consultations have taken place and a model law on refugees has been drafted by Indian Group of Concerned Eminent Persons under the chairmanship of Justice P.N. Bhagwati, former Chief Justice of India. I was also invited to be a member of the group. Justice Bhagwati has succinctly posed the problem as follows: "Would the setting up of an appropriate legal structure or framework not help to provide a measure of certainty in the states dealing with the problems of refugees and provide greater protection to the refugees?" India and other South Asian countries must seriously ponder over this question.

The basic principle underlying New Delhi's refugee policy is to view the problem in a strictly bilateral perspective. Dealing with the Tibetan refugees, Jawaharlal Nehru listed three principles. 1. India's desire to maintain friendly relations with the People's Republic of China; 2. Protection of the security and territorial integrity of India and 3. India's deep sympathy for the people of Tibet.

It must be pointed out that, compared with many developed countries, South Asian states have been relatively generous towards asylum seekers. As Tapan Bose points out, South Asian states have given shelter and humanitarian relief to victims of forced migration, natural disaster, ethnic strife and ecological disasters. To quote, "there are very few instances when asylum seekers have been blocked or refused entry to a South Asian State".

Why is India not a signatory to the 1951 Convention? Before finding out the answer, let us study the definition of the refugee in the 1951 UN Convention, which came into force as a response to the humanitarian crisis created by the Second World War. The mandate of the Convention extends to any person who

> as a result of events occurring before 1 January 1951 and owing to well - founded fear of being persecuted for reasons of race, religion, nationality, membership of a particular social group or political opinion, is outside the country of his nationality and is unable or owing to such fear, is unwilling to avail himself of the protection of that country, or who, not having a nationality and being outside the country of his former habitual residence as a result of such events, is unable, or, owing to such fear is unwilling to return to it.

The main feature of the January 31, 1967 UN Protocol was that it removed the temporal and geographical limitations contained in the 1951 Convention. The Organisation of African Unity (OAU) gave the term a different twist in 1969, by characterising as refugees those who fled their country "due to acts of external aggression, occupation, domination by foreign powers or serious disturbances of public order". The 1984 Cartagena Declaration on Refugees stated that "in no case shall a refugee be transferred to a third country against his will".

In order to understand the policy of the Government of India towards the UN definition, it must be kept in mind that the 1951 Convention had its origins in the Cold War politics and was Eurocentric in character. Moreover, the refugee definition is done on the basis of an individual while the Indian experience from 1947 had been mass inflow of refugees, whether from Pakistan before and after partition, Tibet after 1959, and Bengalis from East Pakistan before its liberation or Sri Lankan Tamils after the communal holocaust in July 1983. Equally relevant, as Prof BS Chimni has forcefully argued, the Convention "is being dismantled by the very States which framed the Convention". Any talk of accession "should be linked to the withdrawal of measures that constitute non-entree and temporary protection regimes". Instead of "burden sharing," the Western countries are today resorting to "burden shifting".

The question of signing the UN Convention has engaged the attention of the Government of India on several occasions during 1992-94, just before India became a member of the Executive Committee of the UNHCR. The Ministry of External Affairs rightly considered the Convention and Protocol as "a partial regime of refugee protection drafted in a Eurocentric context". As a backgrounder prepared by the Ministry has pointed out:

> They do not address adequately situations faced by the developing countries, as it is primarily designed to deal with individual cases and not situations with mass influx. They also do not deal adequately with situations of mixed flows, that is they do not distinguish between political refugees and economic migrants... The Convention does

> not provide for a proper balance between the rights and obligations of receiving and source states... The concept of international burden sharing has not been developed adequately in the Convention. The idea of minimum responsibility for states not to create refugee outflows and co-operating with other States in the resolution of the refugee problems should be developed. The credibility of the institution of asylum, which has been steadily whittled down by the developed countries, must be restored.

Rationale for National Refugee Law

Before the countries of South Asia arrive at a consensus on Regional Convention on the Refugees, each State should enact a national refugee law. This legislation should spell out the rights of the refugees; it should also safeguard the territorial integrity of the State. Today, the problems of the refugees are dealt with on an ***ad hoc*** basis. However, there are issues that cannot be tackled this way. For example, do the refugees have the right to work? Do they have freedom of association? Refugee law would provide certainty to these issues; it would also give protection to them. The legislation would make a clear distinction between political refugees and economic migrants. And, what is more, it would incorporate the principle of ***non-refoulement***, the basic tenet of International Refugee Law. Article 33 (D) of the UN Convention states:

> No contracting State shall expel or return ***(refoul)*** a refugee in any manner whatsoever to the frontier of territories,

> where his life or freedom would be threatened on account of his race, religion, nationality, membership of a particular social group or political opinion.

Since there is no refugee law in India, refugees are treated as aliens. They are governed by the Registration of Foreigners Act (Central Act 16 of 1939), which is applicable to all foreigners. The Foreigners Act, 1946 (Central Act 31 of 1946) empowers the State to regulate the entry, presence and departure of aliens in India. The Passport (Entry into India) Act 1920 (Central Act 34 of 1920) and the Passport Act, 1967 (Central Act 15 of 1967) govern the entry and departure of persons. Further, under the Constitution of India, certain fundamental rights such as right to equality (Article 14), right to personal life and liberty (Article 21) and freedom to practice and propagate one's own religion (Article 25) are guaranteed to citizens and non-citizens alike. These provisions, it must be pointed out, are in contrast to certain other rights such as the right to move freely throughout the country, reside and settle in any part of India, practice any profession in India etc. (Article 19), which are only available to citizens.

The judiciary has played a constructive role in promoting the interests of the refugees. In the famous case NHRC ***V*** The State of Arunachal Pradesh (1996), the Supreme Court held, "The State is bound to protect the life and liberty of every human being, be he a citizen or otherwise". The National Human Rights Commission also acts as a watchdog as far as refugee rights are concerned.

Situation in Tamil Nadu

A study of the situation in Tamil Nadu in the post-1983 period is a clear illustration to drive home the point that India should not only take immediate steps to revamp the security machinery, but must also enact a national refugee law. There had been number of serious lapses, which enabled the Tamil Tigers to become a law unto themselves. The assassination of Padmanabha and his EPRLF comrades in June 1990; the cold-blooded murder of Rajiv Gandhi in May 1991; the escape of Kiruban, a top LTTE leader, while being taken to Pudukkottai in April 1993; the escape of Charles Nawaz, a witness in the Rajiv Gandhi murder case in May 1995 from Saidapet Special Camp; the daring escape of LTTE cadres from the Tipu Mahal Special Camp in Vellore in August 1995 – the list is very long, it brings no credit either to New Delhi or to Chennai. If, on that fateful night in Sriperumbudur, female security personnel had physically frisked all women who wanted to garland Rajiv Gandhi, we might not have lost a political leader of great promise in the prime of his life. Among the accused in the Rajiv Gandhi assassination case, six of them – Robert Payas, Jayakumar, Shanti (Jayakumar's wife), Vijayan, Selva Lakshmi (Vijayan's wife) and Bhaskaran (Vijayan's father-in-law)-were registered as refugees.

The absence of a well-defined national refugee law has created a number of anomalous situations. Three illustrations, pertaining to Sri Lankan Tamils, are given below. Among the 26 accused in the Rajiv Gandhi assassination case, as mentioned earlier, six were registered as refugees. Judge Navaneetham awarded capital punishment to all the 26 accused. The Supreme Court confirmed the death sentence on four and awarded life imprisonment for three. The rest were convicted for lesser offences under the Arms Act, Explosives Substance Act, the Foreigners Act, the Passport Act, etc. As they had already undergone imprisonment for these offences, the Supreme Court set them free. While the acquitted Indian nationals were set free, Sri Lankan Tamils were placed in Special Camps.

The second illustration pertains to ***Ahat*** case. The ship ***Ahat*** was registered in Singapore and was flying the Honduras flag. It was allegedly carrying weapons and ammunition to the LTTE, when the Indian Navy and the Indian Coast Guard intercepted it. After an exchange of fire, the ship was set ablaze and some Sri Lankan Tamils, including the LTTE leader Kittu, committed suicide. Judge Lakshmana Reddy acquitted all the accused in the case and ordered the Commissioner of Police to hand them over to the State of Honduras. The Special Investigation Team (SIT) and the Central Bureau of Investigation (CBI) went on appeal to the Supreme Court, which found the accused guilty of some charges and sentenced them to imprisonment for three years. Here again, the accused had completed the term of imprisonment and, therefore, were set free. The State of Honduras did not want to take the Tamils, nor did the Tamils have a Honduras passport. The Tamils also did not want to go back to Sri Lanka. Few Tamils preferred to go to West Asia. The rest were, for few years, in "safe custody" in Visakhapatinam.

The third illustration is a grim reminder of the ignorance of Tamil Nadu security officials about the international network that the Tigers had assiduously built over the years. Bhaskaran, an LTTE guerrilla, was detained in the Saidapet Special Camp after Rajiv Gandhi assassination. No charges were preferred against him and Bhaskaran appealed to the authorities for permission to go abroad. The immigration authorities left Bhaskaran in the Meenambakkam airport. Few weeks later, Bhaskaran was found in Phnom Penh, negotiating surface-to-air missiles for the LTTE. What is more, he boasted to the journalists about how he hoodwinked the security agencies in Chennai.

Reports have appeared in the media about how the Tamil Nadu and Kerala coastlines are being used by undesirable elements to transport Sri Lankan nationals to Australia. It is very likely that some of these Tamils belong to the hard core of the LTTE. The Sri Lankan nationals use small boats to reach the high seas and then are transported to ships manned by lumpen traffickers. Obviously something is seriously amiss with our coastal security. Unless steps are taken to plug the loopholes and beef up the security apparatus, southern districts of Tamil Nadu and Kerala, which were so far considered to be tranquil, may turn out to be danger zones. It is also essential that the State Governments win over the fishermen to their side so that they become the eyes and ears of the government in matters concerning national security.

The examples given above should serve as a warning to New Delhi and to Chennai. Even under existing rules and regulations, aliens working against national interests can be deported. There are also judicial precedents. In ***Mohammad Sadiq V The Government of India,*** the Court ordered the deportation of refugees under the Foreigners Act, 1946 since they had engaged in anti-national activities. What is lacking is the political will to take decisive decisions. India, especially Tamil Nadu, cannot afford to be a "soft state". A national legislation on the refugees, combining the humanitarian needs of the refugees and the security interests of the State, should be immediately enacted.

❐

7
When will the Refugees Return to Sri Lanka?

> Refugee problem may often seem intractable but they are not insoluble. In our experience there are two basic pre-requisites for solution; the political will of leaders to tackle the causes and to settle for peace and international determination to push for peace and then to consolidate it. Consolidating peace means helping societies emerging from war to reintegrate refugees in safety and dignity, to rebuild their institutions – including in the field of justice and human rights and to resume their economic development.
>
> **—Sadako Ogata**

"How long may we stay in another man's land?" sang Kasi Ananthan, the Poet Laureate of Tamil Eelam, a few years ago, in a poem which begins with the words: "The parrot and the woodpecker may return to their nest without hindrance, but we the Tamil refugees may not".

Kasi Ananthan, who lives in Tamil Nadu, was a devoted follower of Velupillai Prabhakaran and was passionately committed to the establishment of an independent Tamil Eelam. To the dismay and disappointment of LTTE supporters, the Sri Lankan Army got the upper hand during the Fourth Eelam War. The tide began to turn against the Tigers and a crushing defeat was inflicted on them. Most of its leaders, including Prabhakaran, were killed. The most tragic consequence must be highlighted: Tamil struggle for safety and dignity has been pushed back by several decades.

After the war, the Sri Lankan Government devoted its attention to the rehabilitation of thousands of internally displaced persons. Simultaneously de-mining operations started in war-affected areas. The army presence was gradually reduced and the land which came under high security zones was given back to the owners. The Eastern Province was first declared to be a "cleared area", then the Northern Province was also made suitable for habitation. During the initial years, Sri Lankan Government spokesmen argued that their first priority was to tackle the problems faced by the Internally Displaced Persons. The return of the refugees from Tamil Nadu would be taken up subsequently.

Organisations involved in Repatriation

The organisations involved in the repatriation process - the Government of Tamil Nadu, Sri Lankan Deputy High Commission in Chennai and UNHCR offices in Chennai and in Colombo began to take steps to facilitate the return of refugees to Sri Lanka. The Sri Lankan Deputy High Commission in Chennai has speeded up the process of issuing passports to the needy and issue of marriage and birth certificates. The Government of India has delegated the power to issue the exit permits to local authorities. The UNHCR provides free air tickets from Chennai to Colombo or Tiruchi to Colombo and allows the refugees to carry 50 kgs of goods free of charge. The UNHCR also provides Rs. 750 per person for local transport. The UNHCR office in Colombo receives them and facilitates their return to the native villages. The UNHCR office in Colombo also regularly provides information whether the villages to which the refugees belong are safe for habitation. Naturally, the first movement of refugees was to the Eastern Province; subsequently, the Northern Province was also declared a "cleared area".

Only A Trickle Return

Despite all the welcome initiatives taken by concerned authorities, the return of refugees is taking place at a very slow pace. According to statistics provided by the UNHCR office in Chennai (UNHCR assistance commenced in 2002), the graph, given below, provides the data relating to the return of the refugees to Sri Lanka from 2002 to 2018.

Individuals returned with UNHCR assistance

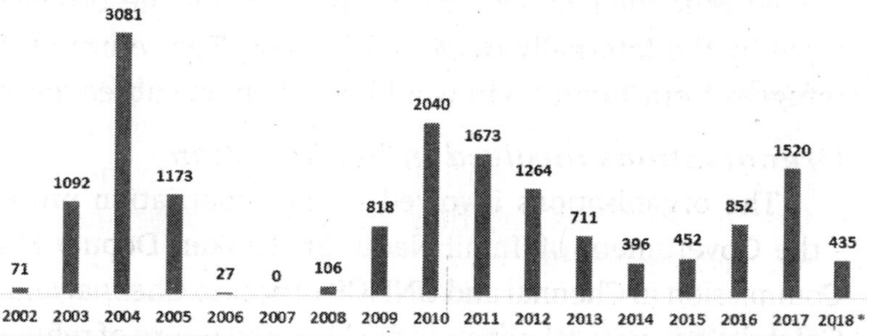

*Data till April 2018
Source: UNHCR Chennai

My conversations with the concerned refugees made it apparent that only those who have land and other means of livelihood in Sri Lanka are opting to return. Most of the refugees are landless labourers and they do not want to go back to Sri Lanka, where there is no certainty of employment nor prospects of owning a house.

The OfERR (Organisation for Eelam Refugees Rehabilitation) maintains that, if the shipping service resumes between Rameshwaram and Talaimannar, return of the refugees can be speeded up. Shipping service should immediately be resumed because it would give a fillip to trade and also tourism. From the refugee point of view, they believe that they will be able to carry all their belongings to Sri Lanka, free of cost. Government of India permitted them to do so when the refugees returned after the India-Sri Lanka Accord of 1987. In fact, it may be mentioned that unscrupulous merchants made use of the refugees and sent through them large number of ***lungies*** on payment of a small commission.

During their stay in India the refugees have accumulated lot of things – almirahs, tables, chairs, fans, bicycles, scooters, sewing machines and gas stoves. They would like to take them back to Sri Lanka. Selling them may be easy in India, but buying them anew in Sri Lanka may not be feasible. While resumption of shipping service will be an additional incentive, the return of the refugees mainly hinges upon a home to stay and availability of jobs for all able-bodied people. The refugees are in touch with their friends and relatives in Sri Lanka and they know that homes and jobs are not easily available.

Tamil Nadu Situation

The situation in Tamil Nadu is very congenial for the continued stay of refugees. Neither the Government nor the opposition parties have so far raised the issue of the return of the refugees to Sri Lanka. In fact, occasionally political parties have declared that facilities should be provided to Sri Lankan refugees to acquire Indian citizenship. It is unfortunate that the current debate revolves around what

India can do to assist the refugees but there is not much discussion about what Sri Lanka, the refugee generating country, can do to assist the returnees. The need of the hour is for the Government of Sri Lanka to do a survey of manpower requirements in the Northern and Eastern Provinces, and link them with training programmes in the refugee camps. The Government of Sri Lanka, in co-operation with the Central and State Government in India and international organizations, can start training programmes in the camps in cases like carpenters, masons, electricians, welders, para-medical personnel. Refugees could be trained in these professions and they could be meaningfully absorbed once they return to Sri Lanka.

When the displaced persons from Pakistan began to pour into India, the Central and State governments, for a period of 50 years, provided reservations for the displaced persons in recruitment of jobs, admissions to educational institutions and allotment of homes. The Sri Lankan Government could emulate this precedent.

Sri Lanka can also draw lessons from India's past failures. When the Sirimavo-Shastri Pact was signed in October 1964, it was apparent that thousands of Indian Tamils would become Indian citizens and would return to India. The rehabilitation of the Indian citizens started in 1968 and continued till July 1983. New Delhi could have provided training to these people in various skills, so that when they returned to India, they could have become productive citizens. However, what happened was a tragic story. Except for the miniscule number who were absorbed in government owned tea plantations, nearly 80 per cent of the repatriates were provided with business loans, loan amounting to Rs. 5000. The repatriates had no business acumen, their business ventures failed and they moved to Nilgiris and Kodaikanal as bonded labourers. For the repatriates it was a bitter homecoming. Let not history turn an accusing finger and remind us, as T S Eliot has done in the ***Four Quartets,*** "We had the experience, but missed the meaning".

Competitive Politics in Tamil Nadu – Impact on Refugees

When the Fourth Eelam War was at its peak, the DMK was in power in Tamil Nadu, it also shared power with the Centre. There was understandable criticism directed against the Chief Minister that he did precious little to safeguard the lives of the innocent Tamils who were caught between the Lions and the Tigers. The political gimmicks of the Chief Minister – the hunger strike which started after breakfast and concluded before lunch – could not save the lives of thousands of innocent Tamils.

After the war was over, the DMK wanted to redeem its honour by showing extraordinary interest in the plight of the refugees. Participating in the concluding session of the birthday centenary celebrations of C.N. Annadurai, Karunanidhi demanded that the Sri Lankan refugees living in and outside the camps should be given Indian citizenship. When it was pointed out that the issue of citizenship was riddled with several dilemmas, Karunanidhi quietly dropped the issue. In subsequent statements, Karunaniidhi changed track and said that the refugees should be accorded the status of permanent residents.

The expectation of sections of refugees was reflected in a statement issued by K. Satchidanandan to the Tamil edition of ***India Today:***

> We do not want Indian citizenship nor do we want dual citizenship. What we expect is the same status accorded to the Nepalese in India, so that we can move freely in the country, we can pursue higher education and we can engage in any vocation that we like.

What Satchidanandan failed to mention is the fact the rights that the Nepalese enjoy are also given to Indians in Nepal. Will Sri Lankan Government be prepared to grant these rights on a reciprocal basis to Indians? It is more like expecting the sun to rise in the West.

P. Chidambaram, former Union Home Minister, and M.K. Narayanan, former National Security Advisor, had stated that the matter of citizenship to the Sri Lankan refugees is under the consideration of the Government of India. But so far, no progress has been reported in this direction.

Karunanidhi deputed his colleagues to visit the refugee camps, talk to the refugees and report to him on the living conditions. He also met S.C. Chandrahasan of the OfFER and Satchidanandan. The Chief Minister announced that Rs. 12 crore would be sanctioned to bring about improvement in the living conditions in the camps.

S.C. Chandrahasan, the founding father of OfFER, is of the view that 10,000 refugees who have returned to Sri Lanka are "happy", and this fact would encourage other refugees to speedily return home. He wanted the shipping service between Rameshwaram and Talaimannar to be resumed soon, so that the refugees can take with them all their belongings. He pleaded that a Memorandum of Understanding between India and Sri Lanka should be signed to facilitate the structured return of the refugees with aid packages provided to them.

Chandrahasan added:

> There is total security and employment opportunities to re-build their lives, They could reclaim their lands, find jobs, and, above all, have the satisfaction of living in their own country, as full-fledged citizens.

Chandrahasan thanked India and Tamil Nadu for generous gestures:

> India and Tamil Nadu took care of us well and we will be ever grateful to our hosts; but we must go back without further delay, instead of falling prey to unscrupulous agents and undertaking perilous boat trips seeking greener pastures in distant countries like Australia where entry is not possible.

Perceptive Indian journalists, who know Sri Lanka very well, do not share the sense of optimism that Chandrahasan wants to convey. R.K. Radhakrishnan, on the basis of information provided by knowledgeable Sri Lankans, has written in the ***Frontline:***

> There are not many happy endings among the 315 refugee families who have gone back in 2015. "Their lot is really bad. Most are staying with relatives and friends and are trying to pick up the threads in their lives", said an official who monitors the situation in the Northern Province. Asked if there are any success stories he

> said that he had not come across any. Instead, instances of repatriated refugees asking to go back to India were increasing.

It is reliably learnt that few refugees, who got repatriated to Sri Lanka with high hopes have returned to Tamil Nadu through illegal means. They hoped that they will be registered as refugees again and would be admitted to the refugee camps. Existing legal provisions do not provide for such a contingency. They live outside the camps and work on daily wages to sustain themselves.

I am wary of generalisation and propounding simplistic solutions. One can understand Chandrahasan's point of view, for refugees are his constituency since 1983. There are different points of view among the refugees. Those who want to return to Sri Lanka must be given all facilities to return to the island. What about sections of Hill country Tamil refugees who want to acquire Indian citizenship? The issue is of great relevance because of the recent initiatives taken by the Government of India to amend the Citizenship Act of 1955. This subject will be dealt with in the next chapter.

❒

8

Bill to Amend the Citizenship Act, 2016

> There is something repugnant and abnormal in the fact that thousands upon thousands of human beings are forced to leave their country... transplantation cannot be a definite solution to the situation of the refugees. They have a right to go back to their roots, to return to their native land with its national sovereignty and its right to independence and self-determination.
>
> **—Pope John Paul II**

On July 19, 2016, the Government of India introduced a Bill in Parliament to amend certain provisions of the Citizenship Act, 1955. The Bill has now been referred to the Joint Select Committee of Parliament. The object of the proposed Bill is to enable Hindus, Sikhs, Buddhists, Jains, Parsis and Christians, who have fled to India from Pakistan, Bangladesh and Afghanistan without valid travel documents or those whose valid travel documents have expired in recent years to acquire Indian citizenship by the process of naturalisation. Under the bill, such persons will not be treated as illegal immigrants for the purpose of the Citizenship Act.

In another amendment, the aggregate period of residential qualification for the process of citizenship by naturalisation of such persons is proposed to be reduced from 11 years to 6 years. A large number of people who would otherwise be illegal immigrants can now heave a sigh of relief; if the bill goes through they would be eligible to become Indian citizens.

Background

The Citizenship Amendment Bill, 2016 owes its genesis to the assurance given by Prime Minister Narendra Modi that Hindus from these three countries, who have sought asylum in India, would be conferred Indian citizenship. But, since singling out Hindus alone could be discriminatory, the Bill has extended the right to acquire citizenship to other religious minorities living in those three countries.

The Bill, if passed, would be of immense benefit to Chakmas and Hajongs of Bangladesh, displaced because of the construction of the Kaptai dam, who had been refugees for nearly 65 years. The Supreme Court in Committee for C.R. of C.A.P. V State of Arunachal Pradesh directed the Government of India and the State of Arunachal Pradesh to grant citizenship to eligible persons from these communities, and to protect their life and liberty and further prohibited discrimination against them.

The proposed Bill recognises and protects the rights of the refugees and represents a welcome change in India's refugee policy. But it would have been appropriate if the Bill had used the term "persecuted minorities" instead of listing the non-Muslim minorities in the three countries. To give an example, the Ahmediyas are not recognised as Muslims in Pakistan and are subject to many acts of discrimination. Other groups include members of the Rohingyas who being

Muslims, are subject to discrimination in Myanmar and have fled to India. Such a gesture would also have been in conformity with the spirit of linguistic and religious rights of the minorities guaranteed under our Constitution. Unfortunately, the Bill does not take note of the refugees in India from among the Muslim community, who have fled due to persecution and singles out on the basis of religion, thereby being discriminatory.

Serious Omission

Yet another disappointing feature of the Bill is that it does not provide Indian citizenship to the people of Indian origin from Sri Lanka, who have come to Tamil Nadu as refugees after the communal riots in July 1983. In an earlier chapter, I have given the background of the people of Indian origin and described how they were subjected to discrimination by both the British colonial government and the post-independent Sinhalese-dominated governments. The ethnic fratricide in 1977, 1981 and 1983 convinced many Indian Tamils that they cannot co-exist with the Sinhalese in Sri Lanka. They sold all their belongings and came to Tamil Nadu as refugees.

The ***Malaiha*** Tamil refugees number around 29,500 and are residing in refugee camps scattered throughout Tamil Nadu. They have absolutely no moorings in Sri Lanka. Their children have got inter-married with the local people and are well integrated in the Tamil society. The young have availed of educational facilities, but they are not getting jobs commensurate with their qualification, because they are refugees and not Indian citizens. The refugees from Kottapattu camp, near Tiruchi, with whom I interacted, told me "Come what may, we will not go back to Sri Lanka".

All these refugees qualify for Indian citizenship under Article 5 of the Citizenship Act of 1955. However, their plea for Indian citizenship has been negatived, citing a Central Government circular that Sri Lankan refugees are not entitled for Indian citizenship. In a communication dated November 7, 2007 to the Special Commissioner for Rehabilitation, the Secretary to the Government of Tamil Nadu mentioned that there are strict instructions from the Government of India "not to entertain applications of Sri Lankan refugees for the grant of Indian citizenship". I submit that in the light of recent initiatives, the above-mentioned circular of the Government of India must be immediately withdrawn.

The tragic plight of the ***Malaiha*** Tamils, majority of whom are Dalits, must be underlined. They do not have a constituency in Tamil Nadu and the supporters of the LTTE – Nedumaran, Vaiko, Veeramani, Thirumavalavan and others – never utter a single word about these people of Indian origin. I submit that the Amendment Bill should also encompass the people of Indian origin from Sri Lanka, who fled to Tamil Nadu as refugees.

Another distressing aspect of these unfortunate people must be underlined. In the 1960s they were keen to reside in Sri Lanka and become Sri Lankan citizens; but in October 1964, without ascertaining their wishes, New Delhi entered into an agreement with Colombo and conferred Indian citizenship on them. Today, having fled to India as refugees, and having integrated into the Tamil society, they want to acquire Indian citizenship. Will their demand become a cry in the wilderness?

Conclusion

In an earlier chapter, I have quoted from a poem written by children's author Nicola Davies. A refugee boy, with high hopes, enters a school, but is denied admission by the teacher, because "there is no chair for you to sit on". The boy realised that he had no place to go, returns and crawls under the blanket. The poem ends on a happy note.

> The door banged I thought it was the wind. But a child's voice spoke "I bought you this" she said "So you can come to the school". It was a chair. A chair for me to sit on and learn about volcanoes, frogs and singing and drive the war out of my heart.
>
> She smiled and said: "My friends have brought theirs too. So all the children can come to school". Out of every hut, a child came and we walked together on a road all lined with chairs, pushing back the war with every step.

We will be sensitive to the aspirations of the refugees if only we realise that all of us can become refugees. As Benjamin Zephaniah, the refugee poet, has written:

> We can all be refugees Nobody is safe All it takes is a mad leader Or no rain to bring forth food. We can all be refugees We can all be told to go We can be hated by some one For being some one

❐

9
Life in Refugee Camps

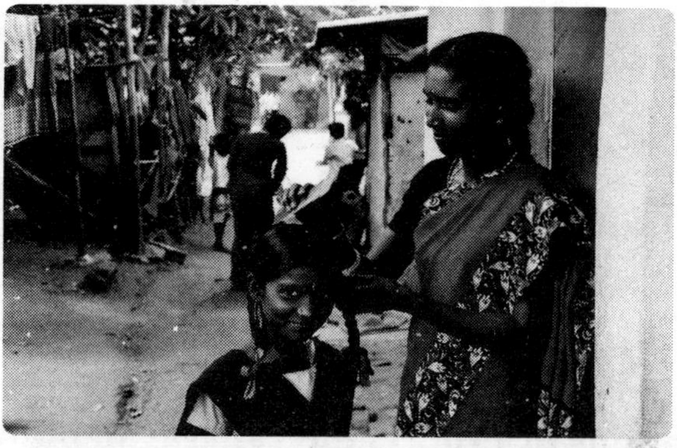

வெற்றியின் முகவரி
23வது குழு

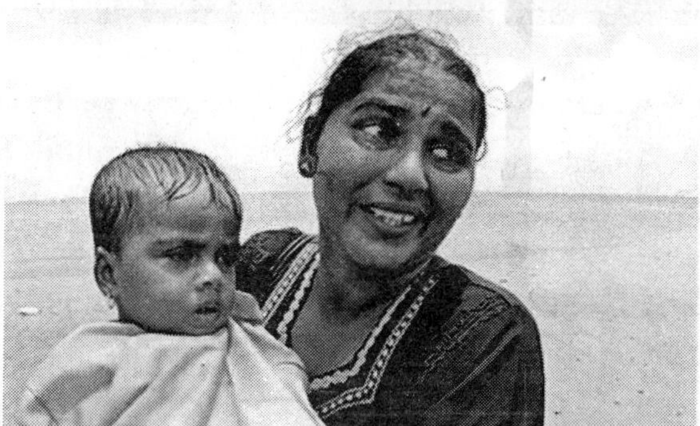

List of Publications

Publications of Prof. V. Suryanarayan on Refugee Issues

1. V. Suryanarayan and V. Sudarsen, *Between Fear and Hope: Sri Lankan Refugees in Tamil Nadu* (T.R. Publishers, Chennai, 2000)
2. V. Suryanarayan and Jacob Ashik Bonofer, Eds., *Refugee Situation in India Today (Center for Asia Studies, Chennai, 2011)*
3. V. Suryanarayan, "Sri Lankan Tamil Refugees", A chapter in S.D. Muni and Lok Raj Baral, Eds, *Refugees and Regional Security in South Asia* (Konark Publishers Pvt Ltd, Delhi, 1996)
4. V. Suryanarayan, "Sheltering Civilians and Warriors", a chapter in Ranabir Sammadar, Ed., *Refugees and the State: Practices of Asylum and Care in India, 1947-2000* (Sage Publications, New Delhi, 2003)
5. V. Suryanarayan, "When Will the Tamil Refugees Return to Sri Lanka?" A chapter in V. Suryanarayan and Sukumar Nambiar, Eds, *Ethnic Reconciliation and Nation Building in Sri Lanka* (T.R. Publications, Chennai, 2010)

□□□